Side Hustle Magic

Discover How to Let Your Hidden Passion Guide You to the Greatest Ideas and Make You More Money from Home or Online!

Gillian Carr

© Copyright 2020 Dellabean LLC- All rights reserved.

The content contained within this book may not be reproduced, duplicated, or transmitted without direct written permission from the author or the publisher.

Under no circumstances will any blame or legal responsibility be held against the publisher, or author, for any damages, reparation, or monetary loss due to the information contained within this book, either directly or indirectly.

Legal Notice:

This book is copyright protected. It is only for personal use. You cannot amend, distribute, sell, use, quote or paraphrase any part, or the content within this book, without the consent of the author or publisher.

Disclaimer Notice:

Please note the information contained within this document is for educational and entertainment purposes only. All effort has been executed to present accurate, up to date, reliable, complete information. No warranties of any kind are declared or implied. Readers acknowledge that the author is not engaged in rendering legal, financial, medical, or professional advice. The content within this book has been derived from various sources. Please consult a licensed professional before attempting any techniques outlined in this book.

By reading this document, the reader agrees that under no circumstances is the author responsible for any losses, direct or indirect, that are incurred as a result of the use of the information contained within this document, including, but not limited to, errors, omissions, or inaccuracies.

Table of Contents

INTRODUCTION 1

CHAPTER 1: QUICK CUT – CUTTING COSTS AND KEEPING YOUR MONEY 9

    SAVE MONEY AND CUT COSTS 16
    A PENNY SAVED IS A PENNY EARNED 25
        Budgeting 27
        Groceries 30
        Saving for Your Business 32
    DOWNSIZING AND SUCCESSFULLY SELLING 34
        Pictures 36
        Other Tips 38

CHAPTER 2: WAIT A MINUTE! – DOUBLE CHECK YOUR CURRENT JOB SITUATION 41

    YOUR CURRENT STATUS 47
        Asking for a Raise 49
        Other Changes 54
    FINDING A STANDARD JOB 57
        How to Find a Job 63

CHAPTER 3: WHAT TO DO WITH YOUR CURRENT JOB 71

    LOOKING FOR MORE 74
    SWITCHING TO PART-TIME 80
    OCCASIONAL EXTRA TIME 84

CHAPTER 4: IT MAY FIT – REGULAR PART-TIME JOBS 89

    THE "NORMAL" STUFF 91
    THE BEST PART-TIME JOBS 93
        Office Jobs 94
        Labor Services 97

	Care Positions 104
FINDING THE RIGHT FIT 108
	Specialized Cleaners 108
	Teaching, Tutoring, and Instructing 112
	Remodeling and Repairs 114
	Expert Jobs 115

CHAPTER 5: QUICK MONEY OR PATIENCE? 119

LONG VERSUS SHORT GIGS 121
SKILLS YOU CAN LEARN FAST OR FREE 129
    Creative Services 130
    Business and Marketing 132
    Craft/Labor 133

CHAPTER 6: ONLINE AND OFFLINE – WHERE ARE YOU GOING TO BE? 137

INTROVERTS VERSUS EXTROVERTS 138
ONLINE ENDEAVORS 143
    Freelance Work 143
    Teaching Resources 145
    Blogging 147
    Online Selling 151
    Testing 153
OFFLINE IDEAS 155
    Lifestyle Jobs 157
    Photography 159

CHAPTER 7: NEED A LITTLE HELP? SKILLS YOU CAN LEARN FAST! 161

FREE AND LOW-COST RESOURCES 166

CHAPTER 8: ALL AROUND YOU – INSPIRATION FROM WHAT AND WHO YOU LOVE 175

STARTUP MENTALITY 178
FINDING INSPIRATION 184
STRENGTH IN KNOWLEDGE 187

CHAPTER 9: HOME SWEET HOME OR LIFE ON THE ROAD? .. 192

- THE CONVENIENCE OF A HOME-BASED BUSINESS 195
- POSSIBILITIES AT HOME 198
- MOBILE JOBS 202

CHAPTER 10: LOVE IT! SELECTION & ACTION 206
- COMMON DOUBTS 210
- SOLID ACTION STEPS 213

CONCLUSION 218
- ABOUT THE AUTHOR 224

REFERENCES 226

Introduction

You and I know the world has changed immensely in the way people live, earn, save, and spend money as we have collectively lived through the recent health crisis. This massive disruption shows us quite vividly how important it is to diversify, and I don't mean if you have a bit of cash in the stock market or a 401k or the like. We have all heard it: That in the stock market and investing in general, you need to avoid putting all your eggs in one basket. You know where I am going with this, you can benefit greatly by having more than one way to earn an income and get it started now. Many people have begun looking for ways actually to engage in earning extra income, but some people just - think a bit, dream a bit, and just never quite act on it. The purpose of this book is to help you find some of the very best choices and opportunities for you and encourage you to move. I know many people who have read several books and spent a lot of time poking around the web, only to get confused and, in the end, just go back to their regular routine. But here's the most important part about you and your future, you want to be able to find that extra something that fits you. It can be hard to see it, feel for it, and then start it. This new endeavor needs to be something that you already know how to do or something where you can quickly gain the skills.

Most importantly, you and I want your new venture to be something you will genuinely want to do. It needs to be something that will work well for you. You don't want to get by with the income you have, and you don't want to waste time or money buying into a get rich quick money-making scheme you've seen on the internet. There are no get rich schemes here, but there are "make money now" choices. You want to find the real deal and the right fit for you.

In this book, I will cut through the clutter and show you how to find and engage in a new "Side Hustle" or Part-Time job that you can enjoy and which could potentially even grow into your full time, absolutely enjoyable occupation. This book will save you time by avoiding rambling blogs and publications that go on and on, with too many stories and tangents that do not go anywhere. I promised myself I would not stuff this book with fluff, or my life story, so I could call it "complete." This book focuses on you, the income streams that fit you, and your new side business that could grow big, really big.

This book will not go on about me whatsoever, I promise, but let me mention, in this paragraph, where I have been. To go along with my full-time career, I have had several rewarding side jobs and startups. Now I am enjoying some great successes and happiness due to my "Side Hustles." But I will tell you that I did not at first. It took time to research, try and fail, and then research and try again. Until I came across the best side jobs and income streams for myself, I tried so many different things that may have worked for some people but were absolutely not the right fit for me. I started my first side job as a kid selling seeds door to door. And actually, I sold quite a few. People certainly love to grow things, and I filled that need.

I have also worked part-time in regular jobs like construction, UPS delivery, restaurant work, and many more. One of the most enjoyable and fruitful things I've done is to create five websites. There are some great ones, and those took a lot of patience. But in the end, they created enjoyment and three of which made income. These included affiliate marketing sites selling posters, Clickbank products, Drop Shipping from AliExpress to customers from a Shopify website as well as selling items through Amazon, called Amazon FBA (which you may know stands for Fulfillment by Amazon). I have also made money buying and selling used cars, computers, as well as many more of my own "startups." My successful choices are not what I want to talk about (I have three other income businesses now), as those choices could give you the wrong impression of what you would love to do, as well as what could genuinely work best for you. After so many trial and error efforts and then ultimately making some choices that brought happy successes, I know how to help you avoid the biggest time wasters and pitfalls. These "time distractions" may have worked for some, but if your heart is not "all in," you could quickly fail with those types of projects, where someone else that loves it could push through. With this guide, you will be able to narrow down the choices to the startups and side hustles that will be fun and beneficial. Your options will work for you because they will be based on your current skills and potential abilities. I have included in chapter 6 a section on quick skill learning with free and low-cost ways to learn almost anything, from Excel to Baking and more. Most importantly, let's find your passion for one or two of the thousands of choices and opportunities available out there!

As the book progresses, your journey will begin to emerge. Topics and ideas will come up that you will say "no way" to, and that is okay! In the first few chapters, I have included a few areas that will help you review your present situation. These chapters will help you decide whether to go ahead and start a new business, or whether modifications to your current job are all that is needed. I would encourage you to read this section as many others had told me this was vital even when they decided to move forward with something new. The review of their current situation helped a few friends decide to stick with it and make a few adjustments to their current employment situation. However, it showed the majority that they wanted and demanded a change in how they earned their livelihood. They felt like the excitement and the possibilities shown in this book allowed them to move forward immediately with enthusiasm and determination. I know that by engaging in this book's journey, you will be able to find the right extra income sources for you. You may find multiple opportunities you like and want to engage in and start. One early word of advice though, start and complete the decision-making process on what you believe at that point to be your favorite idea first. Those other thoughts could undoubtedly distract you from getting started adequately at all. Once you have one that seems to be the right choice for you and it is up and going, see if the other options still "fit in" with your plans.

People have thanked me for how my selection process and encouragement have made a vast and enjoyable difference in their incomes and their lives. The ways they selected their money-making plans are the same ideas and methods of choosing a path that I am going to be explaining in this book.

Your time is valuable, and the income potential is out there waiting. Unfortunately, there are pitfalls to be avoided as well. Many of these new ventures have critical times to enter the fold. Some companies may have only so many slots to fill in a territory. If you start considering one of the more "normal" positions out there, needed spots could be filled and leave you wishing you had started your efforts earlier. If you wait, you will miss being involved early on many of the newest choices available today. Depending on your preferences, you may want to want to be an "early adopter." Regardless of your ultimate path, you must get dialed in now to begin the right actions to benefit you. It is time to find the right income stream and dig in, and by reading this book you have in your hand (or listening to it on audio), you can do just that. I am so glad I took action in the past and will continue to look for options. I want to be engaged in my current activities and yet flexible, and that is what will benefit you as well. Just one seemingly small step, one slight change in direction can lead to an enriching addition to your income, and life. The topics covered in this book have helped people of nearly any age group, from their teens to their eighties, make the extra income they desired.

I am sure you have heard this one: "Some people make it happen, some people watch what happened, and others wonder what happened." I know that since you have read this far, you are in the first category. As each chapter progresses, you will see your income opportunity come into focus. After following this book, it is highly likely that you will soon have a welcome increase in your income and know that you have indeed taken the positive fork in the road. Please be ready to take notes on the ideas that resonate with you. Let's dive in!

Chapter 1:

Quick Cut – Cutting Costs and Keeping Your Money

We live in a world of opportunity. Anyone can start a business.

But not everyone can find success, why is that?

You have an itch to scratch, an entrepreneurial spirit, and a craving for something more. All of this is important, but it means little if you're not first retraining yourself about how you think about money.

A smart businessperson is not necessarily someone who has a lot of money...yet. And their goal is not to just start making money. They know it's going to take some time and sacrifice and choose a sustainable path towards success. And for an endeavor to be durable, this savvy individual wants to have a passion for their efforts. If you are spending your extra money (if you have any) on unnecessary items before you know it, you won't have any extra money. Indeed, not any to start up a new venture that you will be dreaming up soon.

If you know you need a spending adjustment before working on your new goals, dial in this change and get in tune with yourself. Where are you spending your money right now? Where could your costs be cut to allow you to have the ability to at least save enough for investing a bit in your new venture? Some of the startup ideas we will talk about require at least a bit of the "green stuff." The best way to reach your potential is to understand your inner feelings and your personality strengths to find something best suited to you.

Whenever I have looked at successful entrepreneurs and professionals, I have found in their writings a common theme, that success begins in the way you think.

Your deep-seated knowledge of needing to change your situation and just starting down the path you truly want to be on will give you new energy. Your momentum will provide you with immeasurable benefits and motivation for your success.

By the way, I bet we both have a love of food, right? I love to cook, so when I think about putting a business plan together, I like to compare the commitment to success to something I love. Now bear with me here, why not use an example of cooking? Imagine cooking a meal or baking a dessert. Anyone can gather up the ingredients, but it's not just the ingredients and the person cooking it to make the outcome a success. What matters most is the mentality that goes into it. Do you love the idea of making this recipe, are you willing and able to let's say, dice your onion into the perfect sized pieces with flair and love. Do you love seeing how they progress to that particular exact golden color you are imagining? All the steps that go into a great recipe will be nothing compared to the effort it will take for some of the business ideas presented here. So when you pick a new goal, choose one that you dream about, one that has a little voice in your head saying I can genuinely feel this one. Now again, we will be talking about some simple ways to start making money as well. Still, these may not have enough of a possible "dream come true" to capture your imagination for the long haul. Let's not be judgmental if we need a simple solution now, let's make sure you make the money you need if that is the case. But keep your eyes and your heart ready to come across something that you can jump into with both feet, especially that heart of yours! Are you willing to go the distance when you have a challenge? You will need a never give up attitude, and even better, you will need to use your intense passion for that long term big goal for your ultimate success.

I have used inspirational books and quotes, and these can help put you in the right frame of mind. But I want to try something different. I will ask you to have what I call a *"heartfelt mindset."* This heartfelt mindset will not only help you succeed, but you will feel your project as you progress towards that success as well. We both know success does not just fall into our laps, but there is magic in this for you when you are on a heartfelt journey towards it.

The point, again, should not be to make money alone. For those longer-range plans, you will come to believe in and work towards; you will want to have and need to have that heartfelt mindset.

If you know you are not satisfied with your current income right now, even if you have at least part-time jobs or other types of income, we will find ways to add to that income. Today's place is just a point in time; a moment you should only look at as your starting point. If you don't currently have any source of income at all, then that of course, is the first place to start!

You may or may not have been born into a tough situation such as low family income, disruptive family situations, or other challenges that seem like very tough and challenging roadblocks. But as you know, so many successful people were not handed their success. They made their path to that success by breaking through and not accepting their current state of affairs. They made a choice. You may have some of these challenges: Racked up debt from student loans, credit cards, or other decisions you have had to or wanted to make at that time. You could be young or older; it truly doesn't matter. Perhaps you accumulated debt at a young age for school or regrettable purchases before you were able to have a glass of wine legally. Maybe you are older and made some bad choices in friends or relationships. It could have been choices in your location or housing, job choices, or lack of savings when you had a positive cash flow. It may be true that you are in a financial tight spot in your mind at this moment. This could be based on the things that you do or do not have or the things you did or did not do.

Now, it's time to channel your thoughts, to discard excuses. You have roadblocks in the way, but these won't define your future, your choices will. The mentality surrounding the idea that we need money for happiness is only going to stifle our dreams as we go throughout this process. Getting a side job to help for now could be quick. But creating a business and finding ultimate success will not be easy. Still, it will be very satisfying for you, I am sure. Remember, depending on which direction you go, it may not be a quick fix. Often, there are speed bumps in the road to your new long-term goals and success, but that is all they are when you have the right frame of mind. Your new direction and chosen endeavor will come with higher levels of responsibility, and I know you are ready for it.

Money is not just something that we need or want. It is the result of trading your life, measured in time spent working for someone else, or the rewards from your own business.

Save Money and Cut Costs

The first step in making more money is first understanding how to save it. That may sound strange, but you may need those extra few dollars to go towards materials or other necessities to get your new venture underway. Most of us can look back on the money we wasted that we could use today to start up our new side hustle or business venture.

Now is the time to be frugal and a bit calculating with the available income and assets.

Maintaining a healthier mindset around saving money and cutting costs will help you not only live a less stressful life but also make you even more successful. Once the funds from your side-gig do begin flowing, then you must keep a critical eye focused on your lifestyle choices.

Let's review a few expenses; how do you feel about your transportation? What is your current car situation? Do you have a car that is financed? You may be a chronic vehicle buyer or lessee, meaning you buy or lease a newer or brand new vehicle quite often.

Buying or leasing can be considered a necessity. But a careful review of your situation may give you a better idea on transportation needs and expenses. Consider this area first, do you need a car, could you downsize your car, or could you sell any other vehicles you may own? Can you trade it in for something more economical?

Cars are very tricky territory because when you buy a brand new one, it will depreciate or go down in value quickly in most cases. As you know, something like a home is often a better investment. Maybe the area you live in will become more popular. Perhaps you make upgrades and improvements that will help your home's value. Cars are almost always going to depreciate, so it is essential to make logical choices until you hit the big time! If you look to make a change in vehicles try to be very reasonable here, what will work for the tasks at hand? Will an economy car work? Successful people do not often drive around in the cars we imagine, successful people often use careful analysis here and may come up with a Prius hybrid as their best choice, do you think I am kidding? I know many of these people! It is interesting to ask what they drive, and often surprising. When asked, "what is your daily driver," none that I know of having said a luxury vehicle.

Do you need as many cars as you have? Of course, a big family might need two vehicles to ensure that everyone can go back and forth to their various activities.

Could you potentially downsize it to one vehicle? Is public transportation an option? Can you give older children bikes to take to and from school? Could they carpool with other students, or could you carpool with others to work?

Sometimes saving transportation costs doesn't just mean selling our cars. Can you take the bus once or twice a week instead of driving to save on gas? That could be especially important if you have a longer commute and a gas-guzzling car.

It may be an excellent time to review our lifestyle choices. We don't want to eliminate things from our lives, but instead, when we examine them, they could be done less frequently. Think about when you are going out for meals or events. How many times a week are you going out and spending extra money on espressos and lunches you could have brought to work instead?

Treat these instances more like special occasions rather than necessities. Some people feel like they need to go out two or three times a week. Why is it that you enjoy going out so often? Are these ventures providing you enough benefit versus what you're spending? One way to cut back is to continue to patronize your favorite restaurant but order a dinner to go and split it at home with your significant other. That will keep you from ordering extras and getting carried away on drinks and or desserts! If you go to your favorite spot twice a week, pick a day, say every Friday night, for example, and go once a week instead, it will make it more unique.

Put this on your phone's calendar or write it on your wall calendar.

We all love food, but when you look at your shopping logically, this a vast area where we can cut costs. How could you save in this area? How much are you buying, and where do you shop? Do you go to the hip and trendy store, but where you know the prices are higher? You could go to the bargain-priced store for most things and occasionally visit the "fancy" store. Can you look for less expensive alternatives for some of your ingredients? Can you grow some of your favorite items from home? These are all considerations to make when downsizing that burden our monthly budgets.

Do you have kids? If not, I will let you skip one paragraph! You might consider childcare alternatives. Are there cheaper daycare centers you have not checked on in a while that you could potentially take them to? Can you ask a parent or relative to babysit at least once or twice a week for a reduced rate? Consider trading services. Let's say you know how to keep books; you can offer to do somebody's taxes for free if they're willing to help babysit a few times here and there. Maybe you're a great hairstylist; you could offer to cut somebody's hair for free if they trade some childcare services. Consider these bartering ideas to try and see where you might be able to adjust your lifestyle choices.

I hate to say this but smile and think about your debt. The only way to wipe out your debt overnight is pure luck, like winning the lottery. However, there are other options you could use to try and reduce your debt, so you're not giving so much of your hard-earned paycheck to loan or credit card payments.

Consider consolidation loans. You have probably heard about them, let's say you have three different credit cards, a hospital bill, and a few store credit lines. Could you take out a consolidation loan? That would instantly pay all of that debt off, and then you would make a monthly payment on that big loan.

For example, when added together, all of your monthly payments on credit cards might be $400 or $500. Perhaps you find a consolidation loan with even lower interest rates than what you're paying. Plus, it's only $200 a month to get you to reduce your debt at the same rate you are currently doing it. That will free up all of those lines of credit so you can destroy them, or keep just one around in case of an emergency.

Remember to work with your creditors. They are used to ignoring them and not paying their bills, so if you show that you are willing to work with them and have a good history of responsibility, they might be willing to work with you. They might be able to reduce your monthly payments or even reduce interest, depending on the establishment that you are contacting. Consider two different popular methods for reducing your debt. These are known as the snowball and the avalanche method.

The snowball method starts with you, lining up all of your debt, which you would arrange from the lowest amount of debt to the highest. So the smallest might be a $100 credit card debt, and the highest might be a $10,000 student loan.

For the method to work, you continue to pay each of your monthly payments. Then all of the income that you're using to pay off your debt, you would put towards the lowest amount at a time. You would kill off that $100 credit card may be in three weeks, then you would focus on the next debt, maybe a $250 credit card. You would then save and scrape and pay that off, and then move on to the third-lowest debt. This method quickly frees up how many monthly payments you're making; perhaps now you have an extra $50, as you no longer have to pay those monthly payments on the $100 and $250 credit card balances.

The avalanche method works similarly. Instead of going from lowest to highest debt, you would start with the smallest to the highest interest rate. By paying off those high-interest cards or loans faster, you're not adding to your debt. All of those interest rates are continually piling on top of each other. If you're ignoring that, it can be very easy to suddenly rack up even more debt even though you haven't done any more spending.

Another area to review is travel, clothes, and subscription services. These may be some of the fun things you enjoy, and they make life a little more enjoyable. However, they also cost a lot, which can make your life more stressful. Cancel as many subscription services as you can. One method that many people have been enjoying is sharing their subscriptions. Most apps will allow you to do this, maybe by paying a little bit more. For example, you could get Hulu, and your friend gets Spotify. The two of you can trade your account information. You might have to pay a few more dollars a month because you're sharing it with multiple people, but that just means you're saving money by not paying for that second subscription service.

You can also try switching them out month to month. Every month maybe you pay $10 - $20 a month or so to Netflix, Hulu, Disney Plus, and Amazon Prime. Why not instead say, "For June, we'll have Netflix, for July we'll have Hulu, and for August, we'll have Amazon Prime." There are hundreds and hundreds of titles on each of these subscription services, and new ones get added monthly as well. There's no doubt that there's enough for you to watch on any one of these subscription services for a month t a time.

Consider your utilities, like cable and internet. These companies are willing to work with you, just as debtors and lenders are. Bundle your insurances. The more that you can cut these things down, the more money that you will save in the end.

A Penny Saved is a Penny Earned

"A penny saved is a penny earned," is a quote often attributed to Benjamin Franklin. But, he never said that. Instead, in Poor Richard's Almanac, he stated, "A penny saved is two pence clear (Your Dictionary, n.d.).

Regardless of the words explicitly used, we can still take value from this kind of message. Essentially, by not spending money, you're making more in the long run.

On the one hand, be careful, many people justify buying something else when they cut an expense. It could go towards something like saving for your long term plan or buying materials for things you could make and sell on Etsy, for example. On the other, it could legitimately earn you money by sitting in a savings account earning interest while you make your plans.

Remember, little things add up like crazy. Let's say you only pay $200 a month on your electricity bill. It might not seem like that much, especially if you're bringing in, let's say $4,000 a month and your expenses are less than that. However, it can genuinely add up over the years.

It's not just about one specific cost but also that savings mentality that will trickle into your overall planning and spending.

Again, the example of your electricity bill might not be that difficult for you to pay, but then you're ignoring the potential for savings over time. Every instance where you leave a light on in a room that you've left or choose to keep other items on, such as outdoor lights, computers, and other expenses, you're making a decision that you do not plan to improve your finances, and I know you do! The more frugal you can be in every area, the more natural that mentality becomes, and it will spread to all areas of your life.

Budgeting

What are these things that have been keeping us from "earning" more money?

One of the most significant issues people have with money is not setting a budget. It sounds dull, but lacking that structural outline for where your finances should go can be one of the biggest reasons you're struggling to keep your budget in line. Your budget could be broken down by percentages. Probably the best way to start is by listing all monthly or weekly expenses that you have by priority. At the top will be things you can't avoid, and will likely be your rent or mortgage, and below that will be utilities. These are priorities because if you don't pay your electric bill, your electricity gets shut off. We all know we must take care of those needs at the very top first.

Next, you'll consider food and then any other essential products and services. These items could be prescription medications, daycare expenses, perhaps gasoline, and so on. These are necessary costs from week to week that you can group together on your list of expenses.

Next, you'll want to take a look at your income and the mandatory expenses you have written down for your budget. If you run a business or are a freelancer, you might not have an exact idea of how much money you're going to be making. Instead, your budget might be how much you're estimating your income will be.

If you have a salary job where you know every day you're going to be getting $600 a week or $2,400 a month, then it's easier to sort of plan for that and break it down based on your needs, and then figure out how much should be going into each of those areas.

A simple two-column chart drawn on a piece of paper is often the easiest way to look at your situation. On one side, you have your income, and on the other side, your mandatory expenses. Remember to put must pay items at the top. Then comes the hard part, finding areas to cut. Cable TV, Different cell phone plans, and everything on the expense column should be up for review. Even those who are better off financially know that reviewing and cutting costs are an essential step in working towards financial independence.

Groceries

One trick you can use for saving money when shopping is to put at least two items back before you check out. Before even going to the grocery store, you should create a detailed list. The best way to do this is to write everything down, and then consider the layout of the grocery store you will be visiting.

Produce is in one area, dairy is in another. Canned goods, box goods, beverages, cleaning supplies, and things like that all have their isle. Some people even create a map of the store and then create their list based on the path that they're going to take through the grocery store. By doing this, it's easier to avoid those impulsive decisions.

Then, before you check out, find a place where you can pull to the side and go through your cart. Some people even add up the costs with the calculator on their phone or bring a handheld calculator with them.

Consider sales tax, and perhaps you would like to round up to the next dollar, and just consider that the price. If a can of beans was $1.60, say that it's $2. Go through and add things up. Then at the end, ask yourself: what two things can I put back?

If you were extremely frugal and only picked out things you needed, you probably won't need to put anything back. At the very least, you forced yourself to reflect on your choices. Or maybe, in the end, you will have discovered, "Wow, I didn't even realize, I put ten things in my cart that I don't even need."

You can then put those items back, or buy them just this once and put them in the food donation bin on the way out. That way, you help someone and learn your frugality lesson at the same time. Just remember if you return the items to be polite and respectful to the establishment, and put things back in their n place. If you decide that you don't need that extra frozen item, don't set it on the toilet paper rack where you counted your groceries; this will just hurt your sense of self. We have all seen items left on the wrong shelf and wondered about the type of person that would do that. It seems minor, but it really will help you have a better day month and year if you have the motto "do the right thing." Of course, we all know store brands are less expensive, and most of the time, it's the same product with the same ingredients, and you don't need to be paying for name-brand marketing and packaging.

Saving for Your Business

When it comes to budgeting, if you are currently operating your own business, it is just as important to also be frugal with any spending outlays. This is especially true if you plan to start a side-gig, which will become a more lucrative process later on.

You can do the same thing for your business that you do at home: cut down costs, consolidate loans, and work with the companies that you are paying to lower these extra costs.

Look at the potential for outsourcing jobs, hiring interns, or hiring online at sites like Fiverr.com or

Upwork.com to help keep costs in line. You won't want to cut your dedicated and loyal employees and switch to interns or these other cost-cutting areas unless you must.

However, when you need a little extra help or have a new opening for a particular position, why not hire someone who works part-time? Why not hire a freelancer who only works when they want from home?

Remember to consolidate costs for papers and supplies. Reduce, reuse, and recycle everything that comes into your office. You can be frugal with workers to show them they need to be very conservative with their supplies. I am sure you don't, but if you're seen not caring about waste, they will also have that attitude when you are not there.

Remember to promote your business through organic advertising. Basic use of social media is free to use, so you should do your absolute best to take advantage of the tools that exist out there. These tools can significantly help your company reach a broad audience, with almost no cost. You may want to get help with some of these SEO (search engine optimization) and SEM (search engine marketing) efforts for your business and or website from a local college student or one of the online sources.

Downsizing and Successfully Selling

Downsizing doesn't mean you have to get rid of everything; it means limiting possessions and resources to what you truly need. Downsizing your fashion budget doesn't mean that you're never allowed to buy a new item of clothing again. Instead, consider if you genuinely need a closet full of clothes that you barely wear. Do you need to purchase those designer brands when you could find many quality pieces at budget-friendly, or dare I say pre-owned clothing stores?

Downsizing also means working with companies to try to pay less. A reminder of something you may know, calling to cancel your subscriptions such as cell phones, XM Sirius radio, Onstar, or any other voluntary services will almost always save you money. These companies have a procedure to keep you as a customer when they receive that cancellation call. You will often get half-price billing for a while, or other benefits may be offered. Downsizing doesn't mean that you have to cancel everything, but instead, you can look for ways to pay less. What one item would you pick (or more) to cancel for now?

Another example would be to go through your closet and pull out high-quality pieces that you simply don't wear anymore. Rather than tossing these or giving them away, consider sites like eBay, Facebook Marketplace, and Offer Up to get the quick results for the items that you plan to sell. You could list them on all of these sites and more. This way, you can have multiple chances to catch the people interested in what you have.

All of these apps are pretty user friendly. The process almost always consists of taking a picture of the item and creating a listing for it. I'm not going to break down all the specifics of how to use these apps here. There are many resources out there to give you further insight if that's where you are struggling. Sites like YouTube have instructional videos on nearly every app and other instructional courses you may be needing.

However, If you are selling, I want to provide you with some tips to get the best offers.

Pictures

The first thing to remember when you create your listing is to take the best pictures possible. You could write a gleaming review for your product and offer it for the lowest price, but if you have a blurry photo, that makes the item look bad. They are buying the picture that you show them. A good image with a terrible caption and description is better than a good caption and story with a terrible picture.

Take the item that you want to sell, and find a clean or appealing backdrop. If you're selling a dress, don't take a picture of it as it's hanging in a messy, cluttered closet. Take the clothing, put it on a hanger, and lay it in front of a blank backdrop. Center the image, hold down on your touchscreen (if you're using a smartphone to focus the image), and snap the picture. Take a couple of photographs. Do not heavily edit your photos; however, you might want to heighten the brightness just a bit or sharpen the focus slightly to enhance the picture.

When you get into this selling mode, go through your entire home to get as many

items photographed and posted as possible. It may seem hard to find the time to do this, but when you have a proper procedure and are on a roll, keep going and get it done!

Make sure that you have images of multiple different angles. Providing just one image does not build value for the potential customer.

People are savvier than many of us would think. While you might have some people who are willing to reach out about these items, they might not be the individuals who are also willing to pay a high price for a quality item.

Other Tips

Gather all the things throughout your home in one location. Items such as clothing, furniture, tools, and old technology will be valuable to someone. Have an assembly mind mentality to get all these things listed…in one day. Plan a day to do it, and add it to your calendar.

When it comes to creating a title for each listing, make sure to use correct punctuation and capitalization.

Create a description with all of the questions that somebody might want to ask. Always check for spelling mistakes. You can use a free grammar service online to check your work before you post it.

Be upfront and honest if there are scratches, tears, rips, or anything else unappealing in this item.

Decide on a price that's fair and reasonable, and that will get you a legitimate offer in return. Don't waste more time than is needed if you decide to sell things, sell them!

Chapter 2:

Wait a Minute! – Double Check Your Current Job Situation

Work should be one of the joys of life, especially if you follow your passion. Unfortunately for many, it is the most significant pain.

Having to work is tough. There's no denying that. Do you know very many people who genuinely love their jobs? Many who do might only be sharing the bright spots and not the most challenging side.

Often people dislike their jobs because they blame that job for the challenging aspects of their life. We have to make money, and therefore we have to work. It is not your job's fault that we have various bills to pay, however with this mindset, what ends up happening is we resent our job because of life's expectations and the pressure we feel.

However, our jobs do take away time we would often want to spend doing something else. We feel that they rob us of some of our passions and leave us feeling mentally and physically drained, day after day. Although it is not your job, or your boss, or your coworkers' fault that you have to pay your bills, often our employment becomes a very sharp point of resentment, and it should not. Many people have turned around their feelings for their situation and become much happier with their lives. With the right attitude about their jobs, people become much more helpful and positive people.

Another example could be your parents or teachers you have had. It's not their fault that you need to get good grades to have success in life. But sometimes as kids, we would get mad at them since they were the voice of discipline. You can make the same comparison to your job. I know how you feel; others have felt the same until they realize that they can set a high standard of leadership that can benefit them and their coworkers. In other words, put on your grown-up and happy game face to help your team have fun while you work. This "rise above it" attitude will give you a much-needed perspective as you branch out to other sources of income, and it will be vital when you start your own business.

We should put our best foot forward every day whether we become self-employed, or continue to work for someone else. Everyone appreciates that upbeat employee that they see at work, and likewise, there may be that person no one wants to be around. Which of these we want to be is our choice, and we get to make that choice every day.

We did not hate school when we had a class with friends that we liked. We did not hate school if we had engaging activities. We certainly appreciated our parents when they had a great attitude. Resentment often comes out when we're already angry, upset, uncomfortable, or worried about other challenges and obligations. Think of that when it comes to being unhappy at your job. Stop and question your thoughts and feelings before you make drastic decisions.

Is there a problem that's going to carry over into the next career? If you don't mind being at work, but you hate that hour-long commute. You don't need to go back to school and get a new degree; you just need to find your current job title in a new location. It's essential to make this distinction before we throw everything we've worked for away and start completely fresh.

We can all help create happiness around our workplace. If you truly dislike your job, and if you're not afraid to work very hard, your current situation can be quite the motivator. It may be the one place where you can find the motivation to start to make a significant change and begin to transform your future into a completely new career.

This chapter is not intended to dissuade you from starting something new but asks you to look at the things you're trying to get away from before making your next big move. You might believe you dislike your job but are there some small adjustments that would make your work life much better? These improvements could be approved by your supervisor if requested, and perhaps you can enjoy those improvements even as you get your other income stream plans prepared. By playing off your current job, you may find a quicker solution to make added income.

I want to be more realistic with this chapter; not everyone will act on their dream. The "magic" can happen for you only if you look in your heart, take the time to reflect, and begin to act based on your conviction in your idea, and with solid dedication.

Do you need to run away from your job and never look back, or could you instead transform it, or adjust it to learn new skills? Could you change the duties to employ your artistry and ingenuity that you would enjoy more? Perhaps your supervisor can adjust your tasks. Is there a skill that you could request to learn that could provide you with better opportunities where you work now? And could these new skills help your possibilities for your ventures later on?

You probably picked your current job or career for a reason. Could there be a morsel of interest in an aspect of your current job or company still waiting for you to play a more significant role? What is it that pulled you into the position in the first place? Question: What is the number one thing you would like to change in your workplace, and can you?

Your Current Status

I want to ask you to imagine a few different scenarios. The first is that you wake up tomorrow and win a lottery of, let's say a few hundred thousand dollars. However, the new lottery rule is that you must start a new business that you agree to make successful or take over a struggling business type that you love and turn it around. You can quit your job and jump into one of these scenarios. Please close your eyes and try this exercise as I want you to imagine removing all barriers for the moment.

What are some of the most fulfilling ideas you could begin to engage in, and what future can you imagine for yourself in this new scenario?

Are you happy that you don't have to wake up early anymore? Are you excited you don't have to deal with the angry customers that you may work with now? Is it your coworkers that you now get to avoid? What would be the most significant relief for you? Of course, not having to worry about making enough money for stability is one. But aside from those things, what physically and emotionally would be better about your life?

Many people will get bored as time passes in a situation where they don't have the typical stability of a job. We are so used to following a routine all of our lives that suddenly when that routine is taken away, many would not handle it well. What would you be doing with your freedom in a world where you could pursue whatever you wanted?

If you came up with some of your dreams that have perhaps been on the shelf, connect those back to what you currently do. Is there any correlation there right now?

Is there a way to tell if you should keep walking down the same path, or if you should change it up and find a new direction?

Ask yourself these questions, and the answer should become clearer: How's work? Do you like it, do you love it, or do you hate it? Could you get a promotion? Could you transfer to a different location? Could you move to a different department? Look at your current status and relate it's viability with your overall goals.

If you have reviewed your situation and at least love the type of business you are in, or at least an angle or portion of that business, you may want to stay with your current career path. There are a few things you can do to try and improve your situation.

Asking for a Raise

Perhaps you have stayed stagnant in your career.

If you are progressing but seem to be taking on more responsibilities, perhaps it's time to start making more. Work-life might not change much for you, but your bank account could change things outside of the office. You could at least start saving up a bit more money, so ultimately if you do decide to leave, you would then have something to fall back on. There are a few important reminders to keep in mind to help you be more confident when you ask for that raise and help you get that raise you deserve.

Time to get out that journal we talked about or a pen and paper.

You will want to go into your boss's office with the reasons why they should be paying you more money for what you're doing.

Maybe you do deserve more money, and that's easy to see from your angle. But perhaps you have a somewhat simple job where you are easily replaceable. Why should they keep you on and not let you go, and just find somebody else? It sounds harsh, but it's a good thing to consider to create a more substantial reason for them to give you a raise. You have to provide them with strong incentives. Start positive and dress for the occasion. Change your clothes, change your attitude, and show up on time. If you aren't hitting all of these marks just yet, that's the first place to start. As an employer, I can tell you they will notice a change of attitude and performance. This preparation may take a few days to a few weeks, and only you can make the proper plan and decide when the time is right. Generally, a few weeks of performance improvement will be a strong signal that you are changing and ready for more compensation.

Create a script and write down your main points for why you are asking for the raise. Always start positive. Begin by sharing what you love about the company and your boss. Remind your supervisor what you have provided for the company in a general sense. Then review where you have gone above and beyond your specific position's duties.

Offer your supervisor an incentive as well. Of course, perhaps you already believe you deserve this raise, and you've gone forgotten in the company for so long, but they still need those reasons to pay more. Could you take on another task? Could you work an extra hour? Could you absorb extra responsibilities from another position? No matter how small, it's good to bring up an addition to the ways you've already been going above and beyond, along with a new suggestion or two.

When you see a posting or hear about an open position in your company, you could offer to take on some of those roles for additional pay in the form of a raise. That way, they wouldn't have to hire an extra person full time. Maybe they would just fill a part-time role because you've offered to take on those responsibilities for your requested bump in pay.

Come up with ideas that would benefit the company. For example, maybe you talk about starting a social media page as an attempt to use organic marketing. You could be the one to bring this idea up and then also offer to fill that role for that improved paycheck.

You can bring up company challenges, cracks you can help fill here and there in the company, and other areas you believe could help.

Plant the seeds, and even if they don't take the offer, it could help blossom into something else. Remember to be comfortable if they turn you down. They might say no and seem a bit annoyed, or things could feel like they went a bit wrong, and that's okay. Perhaps they will think over your proposal and talk to you about it a few days later. If they don't speak with you and ignore you for an extended time, that just shows you that maybe it is time to change your course after all. What have you got to lose by asking for that raise? If you're already considering quitting your job, then clearly there isn't much left to care about at that company anyway, unless they make some meaningful adjustments for you.

Please remember I don't recommend to barge into the supervisor's office and demand a raise or threaten to leave; that's highly unprofessional. You don't want to burn bridges, because they could still be beneficial in the future. Approach the situation professionally and empathetically and carefully handle that possible rejection or a bit of a "slow walk" on the answer. Thank your bosses for the consideration and time, and decide how much time you can and will allow for their response.

Other Changes

Sometimes a small change to your environment could be enough to make your employment situation a little better.

Could you perform your job remotely by asking to work from home? For many people, the same repetitive nine to five type of work patterns can be very tiring. This possibility of remote work is especially relevant if you care for family members. Waking up in the morning, going to work, coming home, taking care of your kids, making dinner, putting them to bed, going to sleep, waking up, and starting all over again can be very difficult.

Taking your job home could mean getting the flexibility your family needs. Most importantly, you could work on your side hustle in your free time, as you are right there at "new business headquarters."

Even if you can't work remotely fulltime, perhaps you could get permission to work one day from home a week, or even just one or more days a month. By reducing the time that you have to go to the office, that could help enough to alleviate some of the resentment or difficulty you have associated with your workplace.

Here could be a helpful idea instead of asking for a raise…you could instead change your trajectory by asking for additional training. Instead of asking for a raise, use the notes you have taken about how you benefit the company and ask for funding to get the training that would help you and the company. Could you take a day off work to go to a class to gain a new skill or a needed certificate? If you can convincingly show the benefit of what that training provides, you may open the door for more beneficial learning opportunities that may help with your future venture plans. It can genuinely make work more satisfying when the company invests in you and more interesting if you get the chance to learn new things to advance and grow.

Also, that training could be helpful if you ever lose your job or decide to leave. You would still have that training on your resume or portfolio. I have landed jobs due to the new skills I was able to list on my resume. Even if you are not certified, let's say in Microsoft Office, being able to say that you are familiar with it and used it goes a long way.

You could simply ask to stop performing some portion of your job as well. Things you bring up might include something that is just pointless. Is it beneficial for the company to pay employees an extra hour of wages, even though no customers come in during that last hour? Is it necessary to host a weekly meeting, even when it could quickly be summed up in an email? Showing your supervisors that you want to be more efficient is always a good thing, as long as you don't appear to be avoiding tasks. Something that often works quite well is to offer a tradeoff instead. For example, you could say, "I think we can save time here by changing the meeting to an email format and spend that saved time with my social media promotion idea.

Finally, see if you can transfer your job somewhere new. That could be in a different area, department, or if you work for a large company, a different location or branch.

The same etiquette applies for asking for this change as when requesting a raise, approach it professionally, provide the benefits, be honest with them, and give them reasons that it is the right time to make these adjustments. Remember, no one else is going to take these actionable steps for you.

If all of this fails and you still end up unhappy – or if the idea of none of this is workable for you - then maybe it truly is your time to chart a new course.

Finding a Standard Job

Although you will be developing a future where your heart and mind are fully engaged with your ultimate goals, the first side hustle you start may not be your end game. Maybe you genuinely like your current job and the skills you use there, and you don't want to change, but it just doesn't pay enough for your personal goals.

For example, being a graphic designer is an excellent job if you're passionate about that artistic outlet and the results you create. You may truly enjoy your work, but unfortunately, you may not be able to earn enough money there. Finding an extra income source that fits you, where you can bank some extra money w continue to do something that you love is a great way to ensure that you're not chasing a dream that will make you unhappy. We will be talking about where you can earn extra money today with your graphic design abilities, or other skills very soon.

A few tips for finding that "standard" job, start looking in your desired niche. It also makes you more valuable when you have that the skills needed or can learn them quickly. If you are a specialist in something, or perhaps even an expert, that, of course, makes you more desirable than being somebody who has less training in a specific field. Consider if you could take your current job and use the skills you use there in a new way.

For example, if you were a school teacher, but you just don't enjoy the "teaching" life t as you thought you would. You could specialize by teaching your specialty as an instructor who gives their private tutoring lessons. Perhaps you can tutor subjects like English, math, history, or science, but a form of art is your true passion. You could then work towards planning, for example, a business where you teach how you create your artwork. Or you may start by freelancing on sites like Facebook after joining art groups. Upwork is a place where you can sell lessons and tutor in various subjects. You may feel like you could have success in providing learning experiences right in your home. You could offer a mobile service and give lessons at the local library (where you can often reserve a room or space on an ongoing basis) or in the client's home to stand out and make learning convenient. You could host wine and paint events, give private lessons for at-home parties, and so on. Get creative with the different things you would like to teach!

Today there are more ways than ever to train over the internet, and it is a trendy avenue to webchat with clients. If you are not familiar with how to do this or have not done it yourself, you could test many online companies Do not be intimidated; it is usually a few steps you can follow and be up and running in no time. Get some friends or family members to practice with, and you could all learn something beneficial. This area of video conferencing chat and remote learning is growing, fast. Companies like Zoom, Webex, Google, Facebook, and more are ready and waiting with free trials to help you get comfortable with their online tools. This online delivery could quite conceivably be an area of business growth for you. Again get those friends and family members to practice with you. That area could be so crucial to your business that you should schedule yourself a day to learn it. I'll wait while you add that to your calendar. Did you add it to your calendar yet? Okay good. That could be an area where you stand out and spread the word on social media, Craigslist, a small post in the local paper if appropriate, bulletin boards, and more.

People don't want to go to a generalist for expert advice; they want to go to an expert.

Starting small is a great way to grow big and strong. Many people have tried to grow too fast by borrowing money and trying to buy their way to success. A person can blow a balloon quickly, but it will undoubtedly pop if it gets too stressed. A seed that gently grows into a plant is something that can keep growing and thriving. You could go big in the wrong direction, and it could be hard to turn the boat, remember the Titanic? They saw the iceberg but were not agile enough to adjust and avoid crashing into it. Starting small allows you to see the possibilities and opportunities better and will enable you to pivot when needed, be nimble.

That is the kind of growth that you want to envision for yourself. You might have to take a lower-paying side hustle, but it could be the thing that helps give you more expertise in an area that you want to pursue eventually. For example, maybe you're working in an office job, and you absolutely can't wait to escape that lifestyle. You have the passion to one day open up a restaurant of your own. You've always loved cooking, and it's just been something in the back of your mind as what feels like just a dream you'll never fulfill.

Why not get a part-time restaurant job or perhaps try to get on as help for a food truck operator as a part-time position to give you more experience with that? You can't go from working in an office to simply opening a restaurant unless you have a large of money to invest. And as you know, going big too fast doesn't work, restaurants have a very high failure rate, and it would be better not to borrow your way into bankruptcy!

Starting part-time in your potential dream field, whatever it is, will give you firsthand experience of what it is like to work in those businesses. You get to answer the question: Is this something that I truly want? You might get involved in a situation and realize you absolutely cannot work with the public all day, and you prefer to be working in a more secluded setting.

That's fine - but it's good to figure that out now because, as a business owner, you will have to be entirely hands-on and face to face with a wide range of customers. In the restaurant example above, I love food too, but when you realize that you dislike the business you have been dreaming about, sooner is better than later. When you're at a "standard" job, you can walk away instead of how it is when you are wrapped up in your own business. With payroll to meet, most likely business loans to pay off, employees, and customers depending on you, there are no other natural options to change your situation. Some people could feel trapped by this entanglement.; would you?

When searching for this "tip your toe in" side job, there are a few things to consider.

How to Find a Job

To find a side job, start by creating a list of your goals. What do you hope to gain from this job? Are you looking strictly for experience, or are you looking specifically to start making money right away in a position already existing? If you're looking to make more money, you have two choices.

You can also get a job solely for the experience. Maybe you're already making an adequate amount to pay your bills in your current position, but you know it is "not you" in the long run, so you're looking to branch out. You might not be as concerned with making money, and instead, you just need to immerse yourself in a new environment. That is why you need to list your goals and what you're hoping to accomplish.

Then create a list of your absolute must-avoid situations. The situations you may want to avoid could be customer service, the food industry, a job where you have to work outdoors, working alone, or in large groups.

Now, let's start to focus on and plan your job hunt.

Why not start your search with a local focus. It could even be something like a walk around your neighborhood's closest business district. What are businesses of interest in your local area? What services are offered and which are not provided? What job possibilities or even new business opportunities do you see? That commute would sure be convenient if work were right there, wouldn't it?! Stroll around your neighborhood and see places that may be hiring. Of course, a law firm might not have a "now hiring" sign in the front window like the diner next door does, but they might need somebody to help answer phones. They might even be looking for an intern. Going for a walk gives you an idea of positions you might not have come across typically. If it is too large an area to cover with a few "walkabouts," use Google Maps street view or simply search "restaurants near me," or "stores near me," etc. You can explore the map and see and connect with other businesses you hadn't thought of this way as well.

People doing tasks will spark ideas mas well. Let's say you see somebody who works for the city trimming a tree on your daily walk. It may give you the insight to start your own landscaping business, for example. As you explore your local possibilities, you may pull inspiration from things you hadn't seen before. Small things can trigger big ideas!

Consider the places where you already like to go. What is it that you enjoy about them? Now don't confuse a place that you want to go as a place that you would like to work.

After that, you

can do an extensive search online. Perhaps one of the most relevant websites where you can create an account showcasing your background and goals is LinkedIn. That is one of the very best sites for making connections for your career or business ventures. The free version is an excellent place to start. The premium one comes with a premium price and better connection abilities for recruiters to communicate with you. I opted to have the premium account at $59 a month premium level, and I found the job I wanted at that time in less than two months, and then I went back to the free version.

You can post a portfolio of your work if you are somebody who has a specialized ability. You may share your skills and experiences, such as accounting, bookkeeping, motivation, writing, photography, or others. You can list past employers and often make connections through employees and ex-employees at listed businesses and related businesses. Often these employers or schools will post something that you can comment on or send people direct messages. Maybe you will find that a manager you worked for in the past is now the manager of a new company who is hiring. You loved working for her, and perhaps now you could get the chance to work with her once again by applying to and being offered that job! It's like a professional social media, where you can become connected to people in your wheelhouse, or at least your area of interest and specific to your employment search. Do not hesitate to reach out to people anywhere to make connections and consider sending private messages about your inquiries.

Aside from that, there are other websites where you can also make profiles and find specific career help, such as:

>Career Builder
>Glassdoor
>Idealist
>Indeed
>Upwork
>Zip Recruiter

You can also use Google Maps to simply look around your neighborhood and maybe even towns and cities not too far away, where there might be exciting positions for you to investigate.

When creating a profile, always remember these rules for success:

Have a professional, clear, and bright picture. Make sure it is you facing the camera (not necessarily looking directly at it but also preferred). Have a natural smile; imagine a friend is telling a joke when someone is taking a picture. Use a clean backdrop like a simple wall, and use bright lighting to ensure you can see everything. After you've taken the picture, ask yourself, "Would I trust this person to do X for me?" X is whatever position you're looking to fulfill. If you were looking for a doctor, you would ask, "Would I trust this person to perform surgery on me?" If you want to be an architect, you might ask, "Would I trust this person to build a house for me?" Be the professional you want to showcase and ensure that is the message you're getting across.

Create a bio that covers who you are, what you are passionate about, your experience, and your goals. Don't give a long-winded story that will bore others. Personal touches are nice, but this isn't a memoir; it's more like a sales pitch.

Include as many examples as possible. If you're a writer, you could have links to your published articles. If you're a social media manager, you could have links to ad campaigns that you would like to showcase. If you're a store manager, you should have a link to the store's website, where reviews are located to showcase your superior performance.

You could write a gleaming cover letter, but it's the realistic, practical aspect of yourself that employers are genuinely seeking.

Chapter 3:

What to Do With Your Current Job

If you're already a seasonal worker, a teacher, or a student, you might be wondering what you should do with your spare time and your current job. The likely answer is to keep it, for now. Unless you have enough money for transition time of 6 months or so without income, then sticking to your current routine is likely your best bet. Even if you have a promising idea for your new side hustle or a full-time job, jumping in and cutting off your current income source could be too risky. There will be some overlap, and being in one of these seasonal situations could be a fantastic situation. In your off time, summer quarter, or other breaks, there is an excellent chance to explore and experiment. Many others must struggle to find this off time to start their new ventures.

For everyone reading or listening to this on audio, now is the time to let new ideas simmer and stew. The first two chapters served to give you a friendly reality check. Do you hate your job, or are you uncomfortable in your personal life and just need to make other moves first? Some people don't need to change their employment situation drastically, they may need to adjust other stressors in their lives. They may need to move to a new neighborhood, simply just a change of scenery, or perhaps work on their relationships to make them happy. Job jumpers sometimes think a new start at a new employer or with a new endeavor is the solution, but if job after job is still not satisfying, there could likely be a deeper issue at hand that needs your attention. The grass is not always greener on the other side of the fence however that neighbor may fertilize and water theirs more.

You will start having more new ideas about what you want to do with your current situation as you continue reading, as well as eliminating things that you know are definitely "not you." Perhaps you are beginning to plan to start a new part-time job. Maybe you have already decided to start planning your own business. But the question still stands: What do I do with my current job? This is a shorter chapter because the answer is still pretty simple: unless you don't need the income you are making to get buy or to buy any necessary items to start the new venture you should likely keep your job, for now. That can be very stabilizing actually, and it may be easier to keep a smile on your face at work as you have something great to look forward to. You can begin this transition into something new, and that is the guide I want to focus on in this chapter. By easing your way into your new reality, you'll ensure you'll have happiness and success and won't end up wanting to go back.

Consider a long-term relationship. Maybe both parties are starting to feel a little "bored" with each other. That original passion and spark have been a bit faded for some time. They break up, and both start dating again.

After just a few months, they're back together. Many people know a couple like this. Often, it's because they didn't need to break up to be happy. They thought they needed a change, but that was not the right change to make. Perhaps the rut they felt they were in was caused by their work situation and a change there could be the new spark they need. So it goes both ways as I mentioned earlier is it the personal things you need to adjust or your professional situation.

If you do make a change, you don't have to break up with your job forever. Now it's time for an adjustment and to find ways to get more from your position.

If it looks like you are sure you want to change things up work-wise, it's time to dive deeper into what you want to get from your life.

Looking for More

Sometimes "more" simply means a career change. Let's look at a few different scenarios you might be in. Below are some bolded quotes. Read through them, and dive further into the explanations to see where you might currently be with your job. Why is it you are looking for more? These examples might help you figure that out.

"I like my job, but I want to make more money for what I'm doing."

You might be in a position where you are happy, but you're just not making enough to pay the bills. This might be true for teachers, artists, tech jobs, healthcare workers, and so on. You signed up for something you were passionate about, but now you're looking for more money. This is normal, which is why an additional side job would be a perfect solution. You could work part-time at your current job ensuring you'll still like it in a few years while also making more money from a different, part-time job.

"I don't like my job, but I get paid a lot, so I'd like to stay."

This means you chose the right field, but something about the position is making you unhappy. This is when you would want to create a new business related to your job or find a new position somewhere else. It could simply be your boss or the company you work for that you don't like.

"I like my job, I make enough money, but I still want more money."

You are clearly passionate about making money, and that's important for continued success! In this situation, it's often best to add a new project. Passion is still important, so consider something related to your current position first, you may see an easier success path along those lines, rather than choosing something that you are unfamiliar with.

"I don't like my job, and I don't get paid enough."

It's time for a big change. Both situations are bad here, so both need to be altered. This could mean quitting and starting over. In the meantime, take on a new part-time job, whether it's related to your passions or not. If you're working an entry-level minimum wage position that you hate, chances are you can find a different one elsewhere that might be a little better as you begin a new side hustle.

"My job is fine on some days, but others are a nightmare. I want a steadier balance."

This is similar to the situation above, about not liking your job. Perhaps the best answer for you in this situation is to search for a similar, but new position elsewhere. For example, maybe you're a nurse in an ER. You might like it on the days when things are slow and you get to connect more with the patients, but the busy days might not be working out for you. In this case, it's not that you hate being a nurse, but perhaps just an ER nurse. Could you find a position working at a doctor's office? Perhaps you could be a travel nurse or a home care nurse. This may be the type of adjustment you need if you do not want to entirely quit your profession, just your position.

"I would love to never have to think about my job, but I am trapped for different reasons."

Maybe you have a contract, high mortgage payments, or even family pressure to keep your job. Now, however, you're not finding that satisfaction anymore. The answer quite often in this situation is to stick to your current job at the moment to keep up with the bills, but start planning your exit strategy right away. Tell your significant other that you will need time set aside to begin to create your side business, and hopefully you will both be fully on board to increase your success moving forward.

"I feel pressured to stay in my position because of all the work I put in, but it's just not something I like."

Perhaps you have a degree, certificate, or another accomplishment in a specific field that provided you with a solid job, but this job no longer makes you happy. Adjusting your duties if possible and beginning to transform part of your job into something different could work, but you should not necessarily give up on your current profession altogether. If you're a counselor but do not enjoy holding in-person therapy sessions, perhaps you could try working towards gaining clientele with challenges that are the ones you prefer to help them with. You could consider starting a web counseling service, writing about the profession. An outlet like that about a stressful profession can often help the way you look at the job itself for the better.

"I like my job, I get paid enough, but I am unhappy."

In this case, something unrelated to your job is going on. Do you hate your city? Do you hate your schedule? Changing jobs might not necessarily be the answer since it doesn't seem like the sole problem in this scenario.

Look at your strengths and weaknesses as you navigate into a new position. What do you hate and love the most about each task you do? The best method in figuring this out is journaling. Write down your feelings. You can also try creating a chart where you can list all of your daily tasks and then separate it into things you like and things you dislike the most about the job.

Switching to Part-Time

Working seasonally or part-time at your main job while starting up your new enterprise is often a solid way to free up the time you need to make your dream a reality.

If you do decide this could work, time the changeover carefully, a well-timed move here when you are ready to start your extra efforts elsewhere is critical. Is this possible for you, to move to part-time work? Could you ramp down, while you ramp up?

If you've been at your job for more than let's say a year or so, transitioning into something new can be a bit stressful. How do you handle stress? If someone suggested moving to a different state, would that stress you out or bring you excitement? If you found out your job was closing and you didn't have anywhere to go tomorrow, would that bring panic or relief? Just because you want to change your job now, doesn't mean finding a new one is going to be an easy transition. Some people are comfortable with these changes, while others feel a bit of a panic as they go "cold turkey" into a new position. You may love the change, while others might want to shift back. The old job provided comfort, so hopping right into a new one, while good for many in the long run, could be too stressful to handle at first.

You can ensure that this is what you truly want to do, and not something you've just been fantasizing about, by making the transition into a part-time position. You can try something out with little to no risks because that old job will still be waiting there when you need it, so long as you stay on good terms.

Going part-time first is good because it makes you confront what you want to do, versus what you've come to believe you wanted. It's easy to gaze out a window and think about how much better off all the people walking down the street have it than you. But everyone you see is likely also dealing with some sort of stressor. Catch yourself in the "grass is greener" mentality, and ensure you actually want to quit by taking things slow and gradually reducing your current job's commitment over time.

You can then quit your job and work part-time while you work on improving that part-time endeavor or side hustle that you started. You will be able to enjoy the end of your past career because that panic of "What am I going to do next?" will have subsided.

This also means that you will work through the initial potential failures of an attempted business as well. Maybe you want to start an Etsy page and quit your current sales job. You could do sales part-time and begin to plan your business and try out different methods of selling. This gives you the freedom to take risks and make mistakes. Without that part-time gig, you might end up having some failures, setbacks, and/or panic attacks. Anxious decisions aren't always the best, so this smooth transition helps to ensure those initial business kinks are worked out.

Be realistic about any differences in pay you might have as well. Yes, you might end up making a lot less at a part-time gig. Still, isn't it worth it if it's in a step in the right direction? You might have to save money and scrape and save at first, but those initial sacrifices will pay off in their own way over time.

Is happiness worth the money you're losing? Is the money worth the happiness you're losing?

Occasional Extra Time

If you have a seasonal position, you're in luck! You will have the chance to be free to try out ways to make more money and find more happiness.

If you are a teacher, consider writing. You can take the subject you are best at and create articles, blogs, and eBooks on the subject. There are always people looking for writers out there, and there are always positions available. You can also consider tutoring online. Doing this just once a week and over the summer could make you enough money to have the things you desire. You can pick different niches, or diversify your portfolio, to try and get new clients. You can also create tutorials or even write classes. Udemy allows many individuals to upload classes to sell to their audience. You can create YouTube videos giving instructions. If you're a charismatic person, you could create a character for the screen and teach kids important things through fun and informative videos.

Students are individuals who likely have plenty of extra time as well. At such a young age, there is so much opportunity out there.

At any age, all experiences are something to learn from. But as a student, this time is more important than ever. Consider first working in a field that you hope to see yourself in eventually. If you want to own a business or go into sales, retail is a great place to start; it teaches you how to interact with customers, as well as provides an opportunity to learn about money management. Seek out office assistant positions for businesses you want to work in, like law firms, doctor's offices, or realtors. You could see if your campus has labs or research facilities if this is an area you want to seek out. Sometimes doing the dirty work is the exact experience you need. You will get a firsthand chance to ensure that the avenue you're seeking is one you truly want to go down.

Perhaps you are here as a retiree looking for a new position. Maybe you want to get out in the world more, or you want to make more money to add to your retirement checks. First, consider working for the community. Can you work for the school? You could help serve food or even be a bus driver. Check out seasonal jobs like amusement parks, or fairs and festivals. You can help assist these kinds of events to be a part of them while also making a little extra money. For example, you could work one day at a three-day music festival and get a free pass for the other two days.

For all of those with extra time, consider any one of the ideas mentioned. Check-in with your goals, and stick to something you know will provide you with happiness, but at the same time, don't forget that making money is a big part of it as well. Don't underestimate trade schools either, if you'd consider becoming a veterinary technician or mechanic. You could get a haircutting license, or become a masseuse, in around a year, meaning you have more specialized training without having to get that 4-year degree. P.S. If you have a degree this is a great time to review how it may be able to help you whether or not it is directly related to your new job or side hustle plans. Some jobs require a four-year degree even if it is unrelated to the position advertised, to see whether applicants follow through with the long-term vision and goals the company wants to succeed in. Things you have learned whether on the job or through school can help employers, possible future partners, or bank loan officers decide whether you are the right piece of the puzzle. Degree or not, feel great about yourself and keep moving forward with your dreams.

Chapter 4:

It May Fit – Regular Part-Time Jobs

It's not a groundbreaking idea to find a new part-time job. But the first place to start when looking for a part-time job is the regular average jobs that don't require specialization or extreme research. This means customer service, the food industry, the retail industry, sales, marketing, business, and more.

You don't have to immediately start a one of a kind, artisanal, home-crafted, handmade business just to make extra money.

This chapter is not to tell you to just give up on any dreams of owning a business, and go out and find a part-time side-gig instead. We are shifting now into providing you with more specific ideas for what your side business could be.

Are you chasing your dream, one that you absolutely want to follow, or are you just following along with an idea because it sounds interesting? Think about the jobs that you've had in the past, and what you enjoyed about them. What is it that you like about those memories, and can you see yourself in a similar or related situation?

When trying to select a job to apply for, first consider your needs or "must-haves". Do you want to only work day shifts? Are you sick of waking up early and working days? Would you rather work nights and weekends?

There are many added benefits, as well as disadvantages, to each type of position that you could potentially get. It is important to review them all carefully to consider how they align with you, and which will ultimately help your long-term goals. First, start by looking at some of the normal "stuff" necessary to help you better find a job that fits you. An idea that may help you, grab a nice clean piece of paper and sketch timelines on them as you see fit. These could help you plan how long each job, each bit of saving, or each course or other learning will take to get to the next step. Use that paper and or a calendar to get started now. Why not take a little break and go grab that paper, or a calendar and write down a small goal on it now? It could be "finish this book by Friday" or start the search for a part-time job after work tomorrow" anything to get started…what could you put to paper at this point?

The "Normal" Stuff

When looking for a part-time opportunity, you may be searching for practical employment, you not looking necessarily at passion projects, although you may find one!

You may decide to start by looking at your challenges. What is it that you struggle with the most? You are not getting interviewed for a job or creating your own business just yet, so now's the time to review what if anything you have trouble with throughout your day. Do you struggle with punctuality? Is it literally hard for you to wake up and go to work in the morning? Are you somebody who works much better at night? Do you like to stay up very late and sleep in really late? How do feel about interacting with and talking to customers?

We often perceive some of these preferences and traits as being negative, but that doesn't have to be the case. Many people work third shifts and function very well. Even though our society caters more so to those who work Monday through Friday schedules, you don't have to live your life like that if you don't want to.

Maybe you are the opposite of that person above who was not regimented, and your strength is in organization and accuracy. Do you like having the same structure every day and do you want to know what the plan is from the moment that you wake up?

Do you struggle to put your happy face on with the public? Or perhaps you enjoy talking to people a little too much to the point it's gotten you in trouble? Sometimes it's best to just find a business where you're tendencies fit properly with others, and that's indeed a great thing.

Be honest and open with your needs, and consider what must be done for you to be satisfied in a position. Go through and list your deal breakers. For example, working only the weekends might be a deal-breaker. Being open on the holidays and having to work on big days of the year might also be a deal-breaker. Having to work on a computer or talk on the phone could be a deal-breaker. What is it about a business or a part-time job that might be bad for you? In the next two sections, I am going to break down different types of part-time jobs that you could easily find through a quick Google search or ones that you can create based on what you are already good at and what skills you might already have.

The Best Part-Time Jobs

Of course, it's a competitive world out there, and you will always have other job applicants to the positions that you apply to. However, this section is going to cover different types of jobs that you could go out and get within a few weeks. These are jobs that don't necessarily require a huge amount of experience. But, again, having that experience sets you apart from the competition. These are also jobs that you could research beforehand, and fulfill the job requirements through your research.

With a strong resume and great interview skills, you could find your way into any one of these positions, especially if you already have some professional experience. It could mean being able to quit your current job so you could transition into something like this while you do work on your passion projects, which might be those smaller, artisanal, niche kinds of businesses.

Office Jobs

Our first category to review is office jobs. These types of positions are frequently available for entry-level workers or those with a little bit of business experience. You could be an assistant that helps with payroll, accounts payable, or even bookkeeping. Many of the advanced positions will require more training or a degree (such as bookkeeping), but there's a good chance that you can get a job like this if your interview and resume show reliability, punctuality, dedication, and the willingness to learn. Employers often just want a good reliable person to train that they imagine they would like to work with!

For example, if you had been the manager let's say at a pizza place, it might not sound applicable to a payroll position you see advertised, but your experience offers a huge amount similarity. You had to schedule people, you had to make sure everybody's hours were right, you might have helped get payroll together, and other related tasks. You can pull those talents from your past position and highlight them on your resume. If you were working at a pizza place, maybe about 90% of your work involved is simply making pizzas and cleaning up after other people. 10% of that still was the office work; you had to go through and make sure that you were tracking inventory and you had to pay attention to sales reports for the day. Your excitement and any office familiarity play a huge role on your resume.

You can find part-time jobs like these by focusing on those skills and talents and making that the center for who you are. When you are interviewing them for these different positions, talk about those skills and what that process is involved. Most of these types of job openings will also list their job duties. They will tell you if you need to do light bookkeeping, set appointments, make phone calls, and answer messages. It will have lists in the job description; you can break those down and customize for each job you want to apply to while creating your resume. Any sort of office experience is also extremely beneficial for you if you are pursuing a more passionate endeavor later on. You might be a very artistic person and have the talents needed to sell products on something like an Etsy page. At the same time, you might be completely clueless when it comes to different managerial operations in a typical office setting. This part-time job you are considering can be seen as on the job training for your future ventures. I can't promise that you'll be able to become an office assistant with no experience whatsoever; I'm simply reminding you that it's not impossible, and if this is something that will help with your long term goals for a business that stirs your passion and dreams, why not give one a shot?

Labor Services

Other income opportunities that you could look into (if you are physically capable) include various types of labor services. There are usually two avenues that you can go down. You can either work mostly with your mind or work predominately with your hands. Typically you can separate jobs into one category or the other. We all know that doctors and nurses work very hard on their feet all day long, so that's one position that kind of falls in both categories. However, labor jobs are more hands-on activities. Of course, it's not to say that you don't have to use your brain whatsoever; all jobs require a certain level of critical thinking.

However, labor-intensive positions might be more appealing to you if you have those hands-on skills and do not mind a physical job. Believe it or not, some people want to be active this way, is this you? It could also be an avenue that you would like to explore if you have been feeling cooped up in your current situation. Sometimes just getting work done using your hands, getting dirty, and feeling yourself work can be more rewarding for some people. For some of us, sitting at a desk and working for 8 hours could be just as tiring as gardening for that same amount of time.

Consider any one of these positions that you could start on your own, as well. These are all jobs that could either be found by doing a basic job search, or there could be potential businesses that you decided to explore. Again, I can't directly give you these positions right now, but I can spark that idea in your mind so you can potentially pursue these one day.

One possibility is helping people move. You could get employment at a specific company to help carry people's furniture and drive the trucks to their destinations. You could also start your own business if you have access to a big truck, and an extra person to help you out. People are willing to pay a lot for movers because it's a one-time fee. This is often a job they need to be done very soon, and you would visit the site and estimate the expense there. Although you may not be the mover yourself, could you get a team together? You have heard of businesses that have trucks labeled "Broke College Kid Movers" etc… could you be the CEO of a new little company that could grow? These are often customers that need help with their move, regardless of the future you decide on, it's always best to find a customer need and fill it.

Another possibility might be removing unwanted materials from customer's homes or businesses. Whether you own a truck or could acquire one by borrowing or financing one, you are simply picking up and removing items customers do not have the time or ability to do themselves. this could be another potential endeavor that you pursue. The same for both of these include delivery services. Again you could invest in your own truck or you could simply work for another company.

Consider specialized services you could provide such as gutter cleaning or window washing. Just like moving, people are always going to need these kinds of services. You can start your new business solo, or likely find positions at local companies. Consider house painting. Whether you're painting the exterior or interior, painting houses is always another business that many people need the supplies for.

Some of these labor-intensive jobs are quite affordable to start up, and much less expensive and bother than trying to open a business with a storefront. Many don't always require that you have an actual business location, but instead, purchase the supplies and rent or buy basic tools as needed. These low startup cost business ideas should not be ignored by the new entrepreneur. Consider the window washing business mentioned above and what it would take to get started. As CEO you will only need transportation, water, cleaning solution, buckets, squeegees, ladders, and not a whole lot more. You should get some training (online videos will suffice) a business license (inexpensive) and insurance. From that point on the window washing business and other businesses in this section are a mostly income business!

Other services you could provide include doing laundry for other people, train to become a locksmith, or even become a composting expert. Consider pest control and removal. You could even be more specialized in these types of services by picking a certain pest, like mice or hornets. Many of these would be great to learn at a part-time job before diving in.

You might be able to find many of these businesses or opportunities for businesses in your area. If the idea of them inspires you, you can get that part-time job to start and then eventually work towards creating your own business. What opportunities are out there in your neighborhood? What service is lacking in your area? Even though there may be other businesses that are available, do you believe you, or a possible member of your future team, could do a better job of representing and selling that service? In other words, there may be a lack of that service in your area, but even if there are similar businesses you could come up with a great name and a new angle.

Another category is the world of crafts. As you know these are items that you are creating artistically. Please do not only think about making abstract paintings or photography, either. For example, specialty candle making is very popular. People love having access to natural, homemade candles with their various scents. Wax is fairly inexpensive depending on the type of wax and where you purchase it. The glass containers that you may be putting some of them in as well as the coloring and scents to use that we might be a little more costly. One great site to get materials and free training is candlewick.com.

If you enjoy that kind of creative process this is certainly something that you could pursue. You can also consider custom creations where people pick the style, color, or another embellishment.

Do you have other abilities in pottery, woodworking, or other hands-on skill? In any one of these possibilities, you are creating something that people can give as a gift and treasure for years to come.

There are other possibilities like furniture restoration as well as other items that can be refurbished or repurposed. You can find hidden treasures at thrift stores, antique shops, and garage sales. Could you restore them and clean them up so they are nice-looking, or repurpose them into something new? Many people like the experience of purchasing something that has a bit more of a story and character behind it.

Care Positions

If you are compassionate and empathetic and have a lot of patience, this is a perfect avenue for you to go down. Not only do these types of positions give you more freedom, but they could also have more meaning behind them. Serving somebody at a restaurant as a hostess isn't always as deeply satisfying as being a caretaker. At that busy restaurant, you may see fifty people a day, and then you could easily forget them after a short time. You could be an at-home caretaker, or work one-on-one with another person, making more meaningful connections.

Perhaps you connect with animals very well and could consider providing pet care, and by the way, some people prefer the term "companion." Business opportunities could include anything from grooming to feeding to simply walking. You can pet-sit at home, or you can go to somebody else's house and watch the animals there. You can also have multiple clients and take these dogs for walks multiple times a day. You could set your schedule to only weekends, only afternoons, or only early mornings. You can work for a specific dog-walking company, or you can create your own business based on your abilities and vision. Another popular business that is similar but requires a bit of equipment but may be workable for you is mobile pet (or companion) grooming. Could you envision one of these businesses as your own? Could you modify or combine these ideas to make an even more attractive service?

A great way to do this is to start by finding a few clients that you already know. This could be friends, family, coworkers, or neighbors. Create a free social media page and a low-cost website advertising your services and schedule. You can include your contact information and rates, and print some business cards from home. Of course, there will be things along the way that will be challenging, so starting small and then growing as people become aware of you is very cost-efficient. Believe me, people want many of these services and with a friendly name, business card, and simple website you will be well on your way. These types of services receive many referrals as well. Often people who start these businesses start small, and in a few months, have that thriving business they envisioned.

Childcare services are always in demand. You could nanny and be a full-time caregiver by moving in with a family, or you could simply babysit on nights and weekends. The same goes for this as it would for pet-grooming if you're looking to start your own company. Having somebody that you know to start is usually a great way to help, and that way you can also ensure this is the direction that you want to go in. Remember to apply any skills you have at your current position to what you want to showcase for your potential business.

Remember that pets and kids aren't the only ones that could use your help; you can assist those who are elderly or disabled by getting their groceries, cleaning, making meals and do other simple household chores. These positions are also beneficial because you are not constantly working the whole time. Some moments you might simply be driving to do errands, or waiting and keeping an eye out as the child or the pet naps. You can look forward to that time when you could focus and plan on future business ideas, or relax and rest for the next step in your plan you already have simmering.

Question: If you had to pick one of the ideas we have chatted about so far, which one would it be? For many people, one may be hard to pick just yet. How about this… take a moment to pick three that gave you an "I could do that!" feeling, and write those down.

Finding the Right Fit

Now let's talk about positions that might require a little bit more initial training, certificates, or other skills for you to participate in.

Specialized Cleaners

This first category seems a little unusual, but if you are leaning towards a service business the following ideas you should certainly consider. As you read these ideas, think about your version of these businesses, what is your vision of a business name or enticing logo and slogan? Could these ideas be expanded on, changed up, or combined?

Some people might hire a company to come and clean their homes such as a "Mobile Maids" service on a week to week basis, but a specialized cleaner or other services are not the same. For that reason, you could make more money because as people are willing to pay this one-time fee. It's also not like there are hundreds of options to choose from to get your air ducts or other specialized areas cleaned or serviced, so pursuing something specialized like this might mean finding eager clients a bit easier.

Again, you can search these companies in your area, but at the same time, these might be businesses that you decide to create and pursue on your own. Specialized cleaners should have at least some experience working with the machinery, tools, cleaners, or other processes that they will be working with. If you are not prepared, insured, and bonded, you might find yourself in a tricky situation. These don't necessarily require a college degree, but you might need to take classes to get the certification. Either way, much of the learning necessary for these positions is likely available online through YouTube videos or other online classes.

A specialized cleaner or service might work with any one of the following:

  air duct cleaning

  pool and hot tub cleaning

  aquarium cleaning

  appliance cleaning

  car detailing

  attic and crawl space cleaning and re-insulation

  slate or tile cleaning and sealing

  wood floor cleaning and sealing

Often people don't even think of these jobs, or that they even need those items cleaned. With the right bit of advertising and marketing endeavors, you could certainly be very busy quickly. For any home service work, get your name in front of all realtors in your area. People do many of these maintenance items when selling their property or just after buying a home. Making connections with nursing homes, apartment managers, and local businesses can be huge for your business. Even if the people you contact about your services have someone they work with currently, managers change, other providers slip up or retire, and during busy times more than one provider may be needed. Give them a card and get their email. Send all possible clients a thank you email and ask them to keep it somewhere for future use. Later you will need to reach out at least once more, perhaps at three to six months to let them know you will always be ready to help them. Guess what? Many new clients are won over this way. When your first client changes to you as their service provider, go a little above and beyond to let them know they made the right choice.

Teaching, Tutoring, and Instructing

If you are good at something, you could probably teach it to somebody else. There was once a girl who quit school in fourth grade. When she was asked what she was going to do she said "Well I know enough to teach third grade!" You may have heard that joke before, but the idea is that you can teach what you know if you plan and execute well. Being a teacher is not easy, in any way shape or form. I'm not saying you should go back to school to be an elementary or high school teacher. Instead, start to consider how you could be an instructor, tutor, or teacher on some of the topics you already know how to do. Could you lay out a course of instructional videos in a better way than you have seen elsewhere?

For example, do you know about computers or television and home technology devices and usage? Especially nowadays, people need help learning about the technology they use. You can have specialized classes that you might host at a local community center.

You could also have webinars and host them out of your home digitally. You can create instructional videos on your skillset and make them available on the web. Think about specific groups that need help that you could reach out to. Many people are familiar with their cell phones' basic usage but many people of all ages could use help with today's tech devices and the integration into their homes. Of course, some elderly individuals might need help on how they can use their phones and technology items to call and chat with their families.

If you know how to play any instruments, that's another in-demand side-gig. Not only are you going to be able to teach others how to play their instrument of choice, but you're also playing these things that you love to play on your own. Of course, nobody necessarily becomes a millionaire from giving lessons, but if you spread yourself across many different platforms, it could start as a side income and perhaps become a full-time gig. You can have online videos showing people how to play instruments. You can have people come over to your place, or go to their home to teach them like so many mobile services these days.

Consider specialized exercises like yoga, dance, or martial arts. If you are quite good at any one of these things, you can create your own classes as well. Consider meditating or even translation services as another opportunity for your side hustle.

Remodeling and Repairs

Remodeling and repairing are also very lucrative business options once you break into it, but to start it as your own business might mean investing a lot more money upfront. If you have the means to do this, it's certainly a side hustle you could consider.

To make these home improvement categories more lucrative, you can specialize in one or two of them as well. This might include basement remodeling. Kitchen remodeling, bathroom remodeling, backyard landscaping, garage organization, and garage floor finishing are all growing areas with opportunities for you.

This is certainly could be a bit more costly endeavor, but you may be able to start small and something you could grow with referrals. If you notice that you're a handyperson and you're good at making repairs around the house, consider getting a part-time job at a local remodeling or repairing company. As you get more experience on the job, you could eventually apply that to your own company later on.

Expert Jobs

Anytime you brand yourself as a consultant or an expert, price points can start going up.

You can be an individual consultant. Consider being a life coach, motivator, or mentor if you have some mental health experience or tips for helping others grow. You could be a social media expert for a company. Who do you know that can help you to engage with users and get a lot of followers. If you notice you're pretty good at navigating social media and you have a lot of followers yourself, this is certainly something that you could become an expert in.

You could be a creative expert or consultant for a company that might be thinking of new ad campaigns, you could be a creative writing expert or writing consultant where you're helping people come up with web content for their page. You could be a business consultant or expert where you're helping people start their companies. You could be a customer service expert where you can help a company reach out to its customers and deal with any issues they might have. You can help people sell things online and earn a percentage, often twenty-five to fifty percent, and you get the items with no upfront costs.

You might be an accounting expert, and be able to help people with their taxes. You could be a virtual assistant as well. Any of these positions will be simple to come up with based on what your strengths are. The most important thing is that you brand yourself specifically as this individual. You might not want to say that you are a decorating expert as well as a writer and a stock expert. No one will believe that you can do all those varied things very well. If the items are closely related though, you could market yourself with two and I would say three maximum closely related services.

While it might seem like the more the better, it's also less likely that you're as good at one of those things as somebody else who is specialized is. Imagine going to a restaurant and their menu is ten pages long. They have everything from pizza to burgers to tacos to ice cream to pasta, and everything in between. A menu with five things seems like fewer options, but those five things are going to be a lot higher quality than a restaurant who's trying to make 500 different things every night. Would you rather order a burger from a place that has every kind of food imaginable, or one from the city's best burger spot?

What are your strengths? Write them down and write down what you feel is a feasible way to provide those services. What could you market yourself as an expert in, and create that position for yourself? You would of course want a website, a LinkedIn page, and social media to help showcase your work and why other people should hire you. A position like this is wonderful because you set your hours, and have the freedom to make decisions that work best for you.

Chapter 5:

Quick Money or Patience?

There are two different situations that you might find yourself in right now.

On one hand, you might want to find a way to make money immediately. Perhaps the bills are coming in and you can't keep up with them. Perhaps you don't see yourself being able to do anything extra with your current income like saving for the future, or the ability to take a vacation.

On the other hand, you might feel mentally done with your job and want out, but you're not afraid to take a bit of time to learn a new craft to ensure that your next endeavor is a lifelong one.

Luckily for you, there are plenty of part-time jobs out there that will help supplement your income.

We have thoroughly covered part-time jobs. Going forward, I want to focus more on creating a lifelong business that can completely transform your life. Again, these part-time jobs are all important for you to consider. If you have decided to take up a part-time job, that could be the training and experience needed to make you more successful in your own business later on. The point isn't to start a big business, but a side-gig that could build into a great heartfelt business with long-term potential.

Long Versus Short Gigs

I want to go over the difference between long and short income opportunities, so you can get a better sense of what might work for you. By determining your needs, you will have a better likelihood of finding something that not only works now but works for a very long time.

Long-term gigs take time. Nobody becomes an overnight success overnight! Your longer-term goals will require extra education, training, trial and error, and hard work. Not only does it require professional experience, but also personal experiences that help to shape and create the perspective necessary to follow that continued success.

Your ultimate goals and the path to reach those goals will require patience. You have to be willing to put in extra effort and hard work for some time with little reward.

Long-term gigs are more than likely better for your overall happiness; they're a way to ensure that you will be doing something that you love and want to do for life. They are also something that will often require some sort of initial investment, whether you have to raise funds to purchase supplies or perhaps pay for some type of education to get the necessary skills. These initial hurdles are surely something to consider. However, after all that hard work you put into your ultimate choice, you could have that dream life where work is not working, it's what you love.

An example is an artist who might want to pursue making their art their main business. You know about Etsy right? Etsy is a very popular website where you can sell many things from t-shirts, jewelry, hand made items and so much more. It charges a commission per item, but it's free for people to initially sign up and get started. You can also print on demand, so if you're selling t-shirts with pictures on them, you don't have to have 500 t-shirts, printed and ready to go. Instead, you can have plain t-shirts and have people place orders, and a company like Printful will produce and ship the item. Your Etsy shop integrates with some great print, or make on-demand companies. You make the design, and leave the rest to the production company to produce pack and ship your product.

Food-related side businesses and careers can be rewarding for many people. Possible business ideas include pickling or baking food items for local businesses. Some people have a family side business growing and selling herbs, vegetables, and fruits to local stores and restaurants. All of this is something that you can certainly do, but it's not a quick fix. If you're looking for something urgent and immediate, do not dive into the world of food.

These are also possibilities like training potential workers. We went over in the previous chapter many instructor-led or teaching positions that you could potentially have, but you also have to remember those require some initial education and experience firsthand. If you are considering where to get the skills and information you realize you need to get your extra income venture started there are a few things to consider.

> Do I need to learn this myself?
> Could a friend or family member help me by doing this?
> If I or a team member must learn this part, are there free resources?
> If no free resources are appropriate, are there low-cost choices?
> Where might I learn these skills online for convenience?

When it comes to education for your new course of action, I think the big question is what is the skill set I truly need to have to get this business going, and where can I learn those skills. Can I learn them on free or low-cost websites, or do I need more than those options can provide. After you answer that you can decide if you are willing to take those steps, are you all in?

A special note about skills, if you plan on having your own business there is one big "must do." You need someone on your team that is going to be steady and reliable for this next topic. Most of you will know how important this is whether you engage in it or not. Are you ready? Someone on your core team must learn business social media skills. For those that do not use these channels, you need to know that in the United States, for example, over 80 percent of your potential customers do. That number is climbing and this is where your customers are. If you shy away from spotlighting yourself on these public sites and don't use it personally that's okay, but you need to realize this is the modern-day newspaper, comic strip, gossip column, and business referral zone all in one. The bottom line to business entrepreneurs, be there. Learn how to start your online business presence, post some low-cost ads, join groups, and more. This is not hard, that is why so many people use it and best of all, you don't need college or any expensive courses to learn to be a wiz at it. Just get a pen and paper and take notes from the thousands of YouTube videos before you are ready to launch your business. You can create a buzz out there even before your virtual doors open.

Just a quick mention or reminder, many skills can be learned online or from your local community college. In a year or two, you may be able to gain a certificate and enough skills to work as a refrigeration repair tech, apprentice plumber, and too many other choices to list here. For example, automobile dealerships hire people with an auto mechanic repair certificate and will pay for your additional schooling as time goes on. The bottom line, skills are in high demand out there.

But now let's talk about quicker money-making ideas. These are the ones that are going to make you at least some income much quicker. Many of these are easy, they're more "evergreen" for all, and they usually require little to no experience. These are simple things that may or may not provide you with that much fulfillment, but they could be the way to bring in extra money that is needed now, or extra income to save for that long-term goal you are cooking up.

You know many of these but let's not scoff at them, these are legitimate opportunities and I for one have earned honest money doing some of these myself. The first short, common gig is ridesharing and food delivery. If you have a decent car in good condition, and you need to make money, you have so many options for working in this field. Uber, Lyft, Grubhub, DoorDash, Instacart, and others will give you the ability to make extra money delivering people, food, or products with your vehicle. Other companies such as Postmates even allow you to simply have a bike to participate and make money.

Being an Uber and/or Lyft driver allows you to get people where they need to go, during the day, in the evening, or early morning, whenever it is convenient for you. You can pick areas of your neighborhood that you enjoy or a busier area elsewhere to get more rides quickly. If you live in a small town you could even drive an hour to the nearest big city and work a 12-hour shift and go home, and only have to do that let's say two times a week.

Again, you might not get rich, but you could make enough money to set aside for a rainy-day fund. If you don't want to interact with people or even let strangers into your car, you can consider something like Uber Eats. They even have contactless delivery options now, where the driver just simply leaves the food at the door for customers. You never have to be face to face with anybody other than the people that you're picking the food up from at the restaurant. Instacart and Amazon delivery are also lucrative positions right now because many people are ordering groceries to have delivered to their homes.

They offer contactless delivery so that you can simply go to the store, look at somebody's list that's been automated on a phone for you, pick out these items, place them in a cart, check out, and take them to that person's home. You're grocery shopping yourself anyway, you know how to do this. You don't have to have a college degree to do it. That's not to dismiss it and think that it's easy, but it is something that pretty much anybody can do as long as they can lift perhaps some medium weight items and walk and are willing to put in the work.

Not a big moneymaker, but depending on your situation participating in online surveys and signing up for research studies could earn you some extra money. If you have a certain condition, such as depression, diabetes, endometriosis, Crohn's disease, or other specific conditions, there are many specialized studies you could enroll in. These somewhat common illnesses are usually the most focused on, which means you're going to have opportunities to participate in research that could not only benefit other people in the future but also give you a nice little paycheck.

Skills You Can Learn Fast or Free

These are jobs that you can learn within a few weeks that wouldn't require degrees or certifications. The more experience you have, especially professionally, the better, but you don't have to worry about rushing back to school to get a side hustle like the ones mentioned below.

Creative Services

Creative services will always be in demand. Robots might replace assembly line workers, but the artist will always have a unique, irreplaceable viewpoint.

Do you like to write and or edit written material? Online independent self-publishing is doing well, and you don't even have to be a writer. There are many online services where you can hire a freelancer to write the book, edit it, create covers, write sellable book descriptions, and so on. Then you can publish them and create an engaging author's page. This could eventually become passive income if your topics are popular and your books sell reasonably well. You can of course still write your own books if you want to try your hand at this craft as well.

Website development is another growing market. Pretty much every company should expect to have a website to be more accessible and user-friendly. It's not easy to build a website, so if this is something you're good at or interests you, it's a potential side-gig to pursue.

Videography is much more challenging, as you'd need to be able to rent or obtain equipment somehow. However, if you're already good at using a camera and this is something you enjoy, you could certainly rent out your skills for events like weddings or parties.

Editing is another lucrative creative side-gig, depending on what avenue you go down. Publications and other writing services are often looking for editors. You could take it a step further and learn how to edit videos as well, putting together creative videos for different clients.

Writing is a creative service that could be a moneymaker if you have the talent necessary. There are many different avenues in this area, you could help people create resumes for example. You could also keep things a little broader, and instead focus on any SEO content. Whatever your career might currently be, there's likely room out there for a writer who is an expert in the field. Script-writing is also a little more popular than it used to be, as more and more creators are making video-based content for their company.

Business and Marketing

If you have ever worked in retail, you've already started some of your business training! A sale is a sale, no matter how big or small. You have to learn how to know what you're selling, and why it will appeal to a customer. If you are good at sales, there are many different routes you can take to pursue something on the business side.

Business management might scare some away, as they believe they have to obtain some sort of formal degree.

That's not the case at all. If desired you can start at an entry-level position and work your way up.

Consider the marketing world as well. Now more than ever are companies looking for marketing experts. We talked earlier about how important social media is to a business. management is also a crucial step. You could pursue any one of these avenues with little to no initial training. After just a week of studying online marketing, business, sales, and anything else that interests you, it will be easier to create an appealing portfolio.

Craft/Labor

These might not be skills you can learn fast, but there are many free resources available that can show you how to go about pursuing one of these craftsperson positions. If you have a garage or any other extra room, you can certainly turn it into a studio. These are fun hobbies to begin with, but you could eventually turn them into a business if you're dedicated to creating sellable items.

Farming and gardening is a versatile craft that allows you to diversify your skills. Whether you specifically grow tomatoes or try to sell a plethora of vegetables, people will always want to buy food. You can set up a farm stand at your own home or take things to a farmer's market. Make sure you obtain proper licenses for selling on your land but know that this is often an option for most. Farming isn't just for food. You could farm flowers and sell bouquets. You could farm snails, bees, eggs, and other animals as well.

Woodworking, glassblowing, and metalworking are also options to consider as craft labor. While these might seem daunting, after just a week of studying various books, videos, and other learning resources, you'll start to feel more comfortable with these. To turn a passion into a lucrative career is truly the dream!

Chapter 6:

Online and Offline – Where Are You Going to Be?

Before the current crop of late-night television talk show hosts hit the stage, Johnny Carson stole the screen night after night as a popular late-night host. With so much charisma on television, you would probably assume that he would carry that over into his real life. But that wasn't the case; he was quite the introvert. What does this example mean to you? Can you be in the limelight when needed? Do you need to work in groups or alone, and are you flexible about these different situations?

If you are more outgoing, you can concentrate on the offline world if desired. If you're more reserved, perhaps working online is where you should consider being, unless, like Johnny, you can come out from behind that curtain when the spotlight needs you.

At the end of the chapter, I have broken down the styles of businesses into two categories: online and offline. Offline jobs are for more extroverted people, as you're likely to be working one-on-one with people. The style of business for introverts should be focused on online endeavors, as this will help keep you working primarily alone, and thus be comfortable with your position.

One of the reasons side hustles can fail is that we are going down a path that doesn't align with our desires. Finding out who you indeed are and how you work best is the most efficient way to avoid this.

Introverts Versus Extroverts

When you begin to look for your side hustle, whether or not you are an introvert or extrovert yourself is an important consideration you should take into account.

If you are somebody who likes to keep to themselves and isn't as interested in being outgoing, that's certainly much different than an individual who wishes always to be the center of attention.

Let's break down what the difference between an introvert and an extrovert is.

An introvert prefers to be alone, and they thrive when nobody else is around in their environment. It doesn't mean that they are hateful, mean, harmful, or grumpy; it's merely about working in a closed space without others. For the introvert, this is much more efficient rather than working on a team. Think back to when you were a child. Did you like doing group projects in school, or were you the type who would instead work independently before bringing things together?

Introverts enjoy peace and serenity. You might struggle with anxiety, and that could cause a sensory overload. Perhaps loud noises, constant chatter, and other disruptive sounds make it difficult for you to work in certain places. Introverts are also very reserved. You might not speak up as often. It's not that you don't have a single opinion, it is just that you don't have a bigger urge pushing you to share that opinion with other people.

A typical weekend night for an introvert might include staying home alone and watching T.V. or doing other solitary activities. There's nothing wrong with this, so if you do feel like alone isn't something you like much of the time, it could be that you are an extrovert, and you just don't have that environment to express yourself. An introvert won't altogether avoid these social interactions all the time, as everyone needs other people in their life. However, you might be the type who would go to a birthday party for somebody else and stay for a while and chat, and still enjoy that social interaction - but rather than waiting until two in the morning, you're going to be one of the first ones to head home for the night.

Now before we review the extrovert's personality, let me mention that I have taken a few "personality" tests myself, and it seems that I like to work alone 75% of the time. But I do want to reach out and make a difference with other people. The introvert or extrovert is not an all or nothing proposition. When you are starting up your own business, you will probably need both personality types to be successful, and you may need another person's help. For example, if you are an introvert, your business may require you to step up or step aside in presentation and sales situations.

An extrovert is somebody who's more outgoing. An extrovert feels most comfortable when in a large group setting, rather than being alone. The extrovert may enjoy the attention from, and being surrounded by others. When extroverts are alone, they don't always feel like themselves. The extrovert might not know who they are by themselves, and might be more dependent on other people to figure out what they want, what they like, and what they are going to do (though this is certainly is not right for all extroverts).

An introvert might keep their opinions to themselves and discuss them later on, while an extrovert is more likely just to blurt them out right away. Extroverts are often driven by these passions, which can sometimes mean they're more impulsive. That's not bad either; taking risks is sometimes the best method to find success. Extroverts are a little more enthusiastic and charismatic and show their emotions outwardly. Extroverts usually prefer to work on a team, while an introvert might like to be removed and work on things more independently.

Reflect on yourself and figure out where you might fall between being introvert and extrovert because that distinction could lead you down very different career paths.

Online Endeavors

Online types of businesses are thriving now more than ever since the emergence of COVID-19, the business culture, and avenues to success are continually changing.

Staying online also gives you more personal freedom. You can travel while you work, wear crazy pajama pants if desired, and take your office where you want when you want. Once your online business gets going, working from your local parks, coffee shops, the library, and more are possible.

Freelance Work

Freelancing is not easy, but it is easier than it used to be by far with internet connectivity. It is now possible to so many things in a remote and freelance fashion for anyone willing to work hard, especially in the beginning. A considerable part of this success comes from creating a desirable profile in the right places to contact potential clients.

One current website that's growing for freelancers is Upwork. This website helps connect clients directly to people ready to work. There are different categories of work, including:

Web/mobile/software development
Design/creative
Writing
Sales/marketing
Admin support
Customer service
Data science & analytics
Engineering & architecture

Not only could you work yourself in any one of these positions, but you could also have the potential to hire someone for your business. If you're trying to start a blog or website, you can hire someone through Upwork to do this. Many individuals are willing to work for very reasonable rates, especially if they don't have much experience. You will not have to hire the most expensive in every category. As long as someone knows what they're doing, they can help fill in the blanks as you lead your plans for success.

Question: Could you see yourself online selling services? Perhaps you can organize a business while subletting much of the work. If you start up a business, let's say a graphic design company online, you are the CEO, and you don't have to be the actual artist. Like a brick-and-mortar company, hire who you need when you need them a job at a time.

Teaching Resources

If you want to tutor or train, you can also find help on any one of these websites:

VIPKid
Chegg
Wyzant
Tutor.com

They can connect you with clients explicitly based on your niche. If you are currently a teacher or student right now, there's no reason to not be on one of these sites. You don't have to dedicate yourself full-time and can check in when you need extra income. Creating profiles on all platforms helps diversify your opportunities.

Udemy is also a growing site where you can buy and sell classes. There are over 100,000 classes there. Using this site could be a double win for you. On the one hand, you can purchase courses if you cannot find free resources you need to gain the skills required, and on the other hand, you can sell courses that you create. What are your teachable skills or skills you could learn? Which of these could you teach others?

Udemy class categories are:

    Academics & Teaching
    Business
    Design
    Health & Fitness
    Development

Finance & Accounting

Lifestyle

Marketing

Music

Office Productivity

Personal Development

Photography

Software & I.T.

Classes at this printing Udemy courses range from $10 to $199.

Question: What business ideas do you see and feel yourself in the areas offered above? Which type of course or even a series of classes would you like to make and sell on Udemy?

Blogging

A quality blog that is well maintained is one of the most important things to have for any company, but it could also be the way that you're able to make a full-time income. A blog is how some people will organically get to your page through Google. For example, think of a roofing company. If someone searches, "Should I get my roof replaced?" an article with the same title might come up. It could be on that roofing company's website, offering a call to action to contact the roofing company at the end of the blog post. It's like free advertising. When creating a blog, pick a niche, and make it specific. This way, you can focus on certain information rather than something too broad and confusing to navigate. Many people have a blog, so set yourself apart from the competition by knowing who you are and sticking to it. There are different ways to start your blog and website.

WordPress
Facebook
Medium
Squarespace
Weebly
Blogger
Tumblr
Wix

Each of these has Pros and Cons. You will want to do some research on each depending on your product, services, and overall goals. The quickest way to get customers seeing your page is by creating one on Facebook. You can create a business page in a few minutes right from your main account page. And remember, as we said before, this is where the majority of people are. Creating your website separately from a site with significant traffic sounds lovely, but the results likely will be "slow to grow." You may be better off starting a page on Facebook growing a business, and opening your stand-alone site later. You can link to your independent site from your Facebook business page.

If you want to start a blog and you're not much of a writer, don't worry; there are many freelancers out there eager to help you get started. You can find independent freelancers on LinkedIn or Upwork, or you can use content creating websites like:

    The Urban Writers
    Constant Content
    Crowd Content
    Writer Access

Create video "blogs" for your website by using YouTube. You can also post informative or creative content. Again, just like having a blog, this could be something you do independently or to accommodate your business. For example, maybe you want to use your garden to grow and then sell your vegetables and flowers at the local farmer's market. You could have tutorial videos, time-lapses of plants growing, and informative Vlogs (Video Logs) to help promote your business and get more views from your channel.

Online Selling

Selling things online has never been easier.

As we already discussed, Etsy is a great place to make money from your art. You can customize things individually to print on demand rather than investing too much initially. Etsy is also suitable for flipping. You can go to thrift stores and garage sales and buy vintage and gently used clothing to resell on Etsy. The same idea and process of upgrading, refurbishing, or repurposing furniture can also work well.

Amazon FBA (fulfillment by Amazon) is another growing business. You use Amazon to list your products, and they will store and ship them as well. They take a cut of the price, but it's helpful because you can do all the work online. Your products will sell easier this way because customers who have Prime accounts are more interested in buying things that Amazon has fulfilled as they get them sooner. Some of the most popular items to sell are:

Electronics and accessories
Clothing
Baby/kid items
Craft supplies
Books

You can choose items based on your niche that you might have for your company as well. For example, if you have a blog online, you could use Amazon FBA to sell some of your products.

To enhance your blogs even more, you could also use affiliate marketing where you would specifically list items to sell in your blog. You could write an article like "10 Products You Need for Your Bathroom." Each of those items could come from different product lines, and you could make a small percentage of each sale made through your affiliate links.

Shopify is a website where you can make your page to sell products, rather than relying on something like Amazon.

Testing

I advise against trying to make money with testing and surveys, but I am including it here just in case you want to hear about it. Many of these testing sites will tell you that you could make up to $300 a day! But then when you sign up, you'll be lucky to make $3. It's important to know because you don't want to waste your time chasing all these sites with big promises only for it all to fall through. You won't get rich from taking surveys, but it could help you make $10 - $50 a week here and there. Many also offer compensation through gift cards, so it could save you money by not having to pay for those items out of pocket. The popular survey websites include:

Usertesting.com

Enrollapp.com

Userzoom.com

TrymyUI.com

Surveyjunkie.com

InboxDollars.com

Swagbucks.com

LifePoints.com

These might only pay pennies per survey, but if you're doing a few an hour while you're just bored at work or hanging out at home, it can add up faster than you'd think.

Offline Ideas

Offline jobs don't necessarily mean that you never have to use the internet for them, but instead mean you'll be focusing most of your effort on offline activities.

One of the big offline side-gigs is any sort of flipping. Again, you can use Etsy to sell these things, but that's usually for small stuff. Think about house flipping or even transforming and improving cars. These would take a lot more work with your hands and interacting with other experts throughout the process.

Airbnb is another growing website for people to list and rent out individual rooms or properties. If you are looking for investing large amounts of money, real estate is a great place to start. Begin first by trying to rent out a spare room. You could use websites like:

Domu
Travel Nurse Housing
Cirtru

Consider getting paid for mystery shopping; it involves signing up through a website like:

    Market Force
    Intelli-Shop
    Best Mark

There are others you could research specific to your area as well. Mystery shopping involves going to a restaurant, store, or other business, and then writing about your experience afterward. You're often compensated for your purchases and additional fees as well.

Donating plasma might sound scary, but there is always a need for it, and you could make money for actually helping other people!

You don't have to get a job at your local restaurant to work in the food industry. You could become a freelance waitress or bartender as a way to make extra money on the side. This way, you don't have to commit to a full-time or even part-time gig, and can instead just pick up shifts as needed.

Consider care jobs as we mentioned as well that you could find through Care.com or Rover.com. Aside from these quick side hustles, consider some of these other offline avenues:

Lifestyle Jobs

Some people, of course, are just plain better at certain things than others. If you have a knack for living life to the fullest, are charismatic, and love creating close personal connections with clients, a lifestyle job might be the best choice for your side hustle.

People are looking for life coaches now more than ever. They want someone who can help them live their life to the fullest. You can use your knowledge and experience to point out where they are struggling in life. You can help inspire them and work closely with them as they navigate inevitable struggles.

Consider motivational speaking. If you've overcome addiction, transformed your life, lost a ton of weight, or done anything else incredibly inspiring, why not monetize the wisdom you have to share? Motivational speakers are often requested by schools

, sports teams, businesses, and more to inspire individuals and groups.

Consider party and event planning. If you love these social events, designing, and decorating them, this is something to consider.

Many individuals are also looking for organizers. You can brand yourself as a closet organizer, or even someone experienced with making over pantries. These positions are beneficial because you'll be able to monetize them in additional ways, like writing eBooks or starting a blog.

Photography

If you own or have access to use a high-quality camera, you can put it to good use and earn money from your artistic side. Photography is always going to be in demand. While it seems not to be as popular as it used to be with the camera quality on phones improving, you can still profit from this side hustle. Create a niche category in which you specialize. These may include:

Wedding photography (from the formal ceremony to candid shots at the reception)

Home staging photographs (for realtors looking to place listings for properties)

Event photography (for conferences, contests, gatherings, festivals, etc.)

There are a plethora of niches to consider. You could also learn photo restoration, which would involve taking old pictures and color-correcting them or bringing them back to their former glory.

You can also sell stock photographs through many different websites. These involve essential pictures that people want for their websites or blog. Go to Pixabay.com or Shutterstock.com to get an idea of the kinds of images you could take and then upload. These websites sell these to people who select them online, and you receive a commission.

Chapter 7:

Need a Little Help? Skills You Can Learn FAST!

Education and learning, in general, are often associated with children and young adults. We think you go to school when you're young, you get your high school diploma, you go to college, and then that's it. Some people stop learning. After that, they think that there's no other benefit or added reward for continuing their education. As an individual who's seeking more significant opportunities, you must decide to disregard that mentality. A growth mindset is one that encourages you to explore new opportunities. Continuing education and "spot" or specific skill learning is often the most beneficial to the entrepreneur.

Perhaps starting a new business is your primary preference for your new side venture. If you are doing this, you should know that the biggest obstacle to success could easily be a lack of education on the main topic you have chosen. We often associate learning with structured teaching, but that's not always the case. If there are hands-on learning situations available like friends or family businesses where you can pitch in, they can provide you with great real-life business experience.

You may easily benefit from other people's successful journeys and stories online. Talking to people and listening to others who have been there before can be just as educational as sitting down and learning in a classroom setting. When it comes to learning on your own, there are a few essential tips to remember before we list some of the free and low-cost resources available for you.

The first tip is to make sure that you have a specific place to learn. Don't try to just read in bed unless that truly is an excellent workplace for you. Learning is work, and planning it as such can help you get better results. Don't sit on the couch with the T.V. on and pretend as though you are doing homework, and remove yourself from casual places where you are too comfortable. Instead, choose a specific location where you can sit at a desk, or at least an in a place you know you will learn without distractions. Be brave and turn your phone down and leave it in another room! Put a timer on, let's say for two hours and dig in. Planning your system will help get better results when you write down your policies. If you change your plan a bit, forgive yourself and write down the new layout and start it.

Of course, if you're learning from a screen, I would advise closing all other browsers and tabs for the two hours of learning or whatever time your learning plan calls. Create this separate space and plan your time, because that's how your mind is going to remember better as you study the information you know you want to learn.

Muscle memory teaches us to act in specific ways without even having to think about it thoroughly. Sometimes, this means you walk by the fridge, open it, and look inside, although you're not hungry. For instance, if you are sitting on the couch watching television or playing with that cell phone as you're trying to learn, your brain is going to tell you to get snacks, check your phone, and do these other things that it's used to doing when you're sitting in that spot. If you have a specific education location, you can move to that place, and your muscle memory tells you to click into a learning mindset instantly.

Another important tip is to make sure that you add learning to your routine. Give yourself that two hours or thirty minutes or whatever you have planned for a day, go somewhere else, and complete that much. Section out this time first thing in the morning, right after you are home from work, or before you go to sleep at night. Have these specific times so you know each day that it is what you should be doing at that time.

If you don't schedule it in, it's easy just to put it off.

The final tip is to remember that learning is not just about memorization. You don't have a test to get through and then perhaps forget the information afterward. Of course, you know the point of learning this material you have selected is to make you more successful; you're gaining experience and knowledge that you're going to be able to apply to the endeavors that you pursue. If you're just doing this to make yourself feel smarter on paper, that's not going to benefit you, especially your goals. Most of these free resources don't offer that traditional type of prestigious recognition or degree, but they can be great for use in your real-life startup.

Learning is not easy; it often means having to pursue subjects that might not usually interest you. However, if you're learning on your own, you get to pick and choose the most exciting things. Challenge yourself to go outside what you are used to learning about, and seek new knowledge to get a full sense of what subject you genuinely have passion. You can often learn skills quickly and start something new, but also add it to the knowledge you gain as you pursue it. For example, you may not love accounting much, but you will likely need to understand the basics even if you have someone else do it for you.

Free and Low-Cost Resources

Free resources will help you get the education you need without having to spend a single penny. Access to online training is available at your local library as well. Librarians are not just about books by any means; they will help you work with many mediums and sources. If you ask a question, they want to help.

One area you may not have considered to check out is to see if there are any universities in your area. Though you might not get a degree, you can receive a certificate that you can include in your resume or portfolio. The university may offer online classes that you can follow at your own pace. Many prestigious universities surprisingly provide free online courses, such as:

Stanford
Harvard
Yale
UC Berkeley
MIT

There are many websites (such as Udemy, which we've discussed plenty of times already), where you can also get free education. Udemy has some courses you have to pay for, but they offer free ones as well. Similar websites include:

iTunesU

edX

Open Culture

Khan Academy

Academic Earth

Coursera

Alison

These courses allow you to search specifically for your niche and pick out things that align with your overall goals. You can also consider other places for free education, such as:

TED-Ed

Code

Codecademy

Carnegie Mellon Open Learning Initiative

Lessonpaths

Besides taking courses online, you can also find a ton of free information through various apps on your phone. First, consider YouTube. There are a few ways to find more methods of learning, such as:

Using the search bar to look up what you want to learn

Searching specific professors who might have courses online

Instructional pages that offer how-to style videos

Free documentaries

Public accesses educational videos that you can access on YouTube

Aside from just watching videos, you can also consider looking up podcasts. You can listen to these while working on other things, during long drives, or completing chores like washing dishes or folding laundry. You can listen as you exercise, or while you cook dinner. Download a podcast app on your phone, search for the app for your interests, and be amazed at how many podcasts there are on most topics. There are a ton of different highly educational podcasts as well, such as:

BBC Podcasts

NPR Podcasts

University of Oxford Podcasts

University of London Podcasts

But for our needs as an entrepreneur, there are particular podcasts such as dog training, craft beers, motivation, business, selling, and much more. Try one out, and if it is to slow or seems not to be a fit for you, try another one on the same topic, and you may love it. I am hooked on one now for my current project, but as I said earlier, it does not matter what my plan is, it matters how you feel about your ideas for your business.

Question: What podcast topic would you love to listen to right now? Could that be your favorite topic, could that be your new venture?

Remember, the library is also a massive source of free information that some people ignore. Signing up for a library card is free, as long as you have proof of residency. That might be a driver's license or utility bill with your name and address on it. The requirements are dependent on your specific area, if you don't have one, just ask!

Libraries offer books for every reading level, but aside from that, there are other free hidden resources. You can use computers there for free internet access. Available as well from their website are ebooks. You can watch videos they make, and they will often host free classes for the community as well.

Look into your local community centers and other public locations to see if they offer free courses aligned with your goals. They may or may not be as in-depth as others, but you could still find training that adds to your knowledge and connections to help you in unknown ways down the line by checking these local resources.

Shadowing is free, and a way to get firsthand experience with a position in which you are interested. Could you see yourself calling or going to the workplace of someone you know personally and ask to give you some firsthand experience? Many businesses would not mind a helping hand that you are willing to supply. You could also go online to see if the kinds of companies with the positions you are interested in shadowing would allow this by sending emails and making a few phone calls.

Merely following the news is also essential for education. You can set alerts from different apps for notifications about anything new. Sign up for newsletters from various newspapers or organizations you're interested in, so you have a daily briefing of any necessary information there is to know.

As you go through this process, keep a notebook or journal nearby. You can take notes and keep track of all that is necessary to learn and prepare for your future.

Some of these website's courses have a cost, and you might have to pay a bit for a more in-depth course, but you will often get what you need from the standard offerings. Remember that you will need what is necessary, so it can certainly still be worth buying a course when needed. Don't get sidetracked taking unnecessary courses, take the free ones until circumstances demand that you take a more in-depth class. Make a timeline plan and stick with it for the most part. Be flexible as your landscape changes, and you see reasons for necessary adjustments.

Chapter 8:

All Around You – Inspiration From What and Who You Love

Who has inspired you more than anybody else? If you had to pick one specific role model, who would that be? Is it your mom, your grandparent, or perhaps a teacher? Is it a famous person that you've never even met before?

Whoever you seek motivation from is a perfectly excellent choice. The point is to keep the inspirational feelings in your heart and mind as you begin and then continue your progress. Imagine that they are actually your personal mentor. As they give you advice and help you navigate the tricky world and endeavor that you are pursuing, what information or advice would they share with you? How can you learn from the knowledge and experience that they have to share? If you're ever in a difficult situation and are not sure what to do, you can also ask yourself what they might do if they were in that situation.

What activities inspire you the most? When, where, and why do you feel the most at home? When do you feel the most peaceful? Of course, many of our first thoughts might be that sleeping or eating is the most fun thing in a day. Aside from that, what activities honestly give you a sense of purpose? What can you do for hours and make you forget how much time has passed since you began? In what projects or subjects do you love to get lost? What consumes you? What are your first thoughts, feelings, or motivations when you wake up in the morning, and what does your heartbeat for when you go to bed at night? What do you dream about, and what do you fear? What are you afraid of losing? What do you seek to protect? What do you attempt to gain? What path do you always end up following in the end?

Look at these inspiring and motivating aspects as you are creating this new life. There is inspiration all around us, hidden in every pocket and corner of the world. After some reflection, you will be able to find this easily, and it can provide you with more than you would ever think.

Remind yourself that no matter how many setbacks and roadblocks there are in your life, you will be able to overcome them. In the end, there is a passion inside of you. Something is telling you to get out. Something makes you think, "Hey, I'm unhappy, and I need to change that."

You have to know how to follow that voice, confront those thoughts, and listen to those ideas because that is how you're going to find the most success in the end. Do simple Google searches of the specific businesses in your area that you hope to emulate. Look up your heroes and where they were at your age. Read people's stories and get to know what others have gone through. Sometimes we look at motivational people and only see their success. What we didn't see before is all of the failure, trials, and tribulations they had to endure in the first place.

Startup Mentality

One thing you can do to ensure a positive, happy, and healthy mentality is to learn how to embrace failure.

Failure is the number one way to grow. It is how we can take our thoughts and ideas, try them out, and figure out what worked best. Look back on your life. I'm willing to bet that you have grown the most from are also the most difficult times that you have ever experienced. Of course, going to school and getting a good education might not have been a bad experience for you. But the life lessons that matter the most usually happen when we have our greatest struggles. Losing a loved one, living in poverty, or experiencing an accident in tough times can feel so negative. But they can often teach us essential lessons when we are forced to confront those challenging emotions. I am not mentioning that any one of these situations is good; it's just a reminder that no matter how challenging things may be, there is always something good we can gain from it.

Learn from your mistakes. You have heard it before, don't keep doing the same thing repeatedly and expecting new results. If you have failed in the past, and we all come up short sometimes, that doesn't mean to cast the blame on yourself. It merely means that you now have to reflect and look deep inside yourself to determine what the catalyst for this failure might have been. What information did you overlook? What did you underestimate? Who did you go to for help that ended up not being what you initially thought? While you can't cast blame for failure, you can pinpoint it back to a source to at least have a more informed foundation for starting over.

To have a healthy business startup mentality, make sure that you don't over expect. Having extremely high expectations can be stressful and lead to disappointment or disaster later on. That's not to say to have meager expectations. Let yourself be excited and have optimism and belief as you go forward toward your goals.

However, being blindly positive can be just as harmful as being negative and pessimistic. You don't want to overlook the reality of the situation only because you're using enthusiasm. Again, that's not to say that you have to be afraid; it's the same as embracing failure. Don't change your perspective on your situation, change your perspective on what it means to make mistakes, and have these setbacks because it can be one of the most valuable learning lessons in any process.

Get rid of the idea that you know it all or that you're better, smarter, or more robust than anybody else. Of course, it's good to have confidence and believe in your abilities, but to have the mindset that you can ignore others because you know best is going to be very toxic. That isn't just the case for creating a startup or pursuing a new career. It's also how we should live life in general;

any individual can teach us something essential and inciteful. Let other people share their advice, and you can embrace the ideas and information they have to offer.

I am sure you would not, but don't feel entitled to success because of the effort you'll be putting in. Often people think that they're the hardest worker around. We tend to believe that no one else understands what it's like to go through some of the challenges that we do. That's not to dismiss your efforts. It's just to remind you that just because you're putting time and effort into something doesn't mean that you're going to have quick and easy success.

Don't compare yourself to others. Perhaps your role model did find success when they were 23, and you're 53, and you are just starting to know where you want to go from here. You can't compare these situations because everybody's experiences are so different. You might have started a little later in life, or maybe you are younger, and you're afraid that you won't be able to succeed because of your age. There are success stories for every age group, and there is way too many to begin to imagine.

No matter the situation, we all have our unique perspective that has been crafted throughout the many things that we have experienced. For that reason, we should not and cannot compare ourselves to others, that kind of ego mentality does not get you to your next goal, does it? It does not help you get to your next step, which is what you need to accomplish. Instead of comparing yourself to others, always look for information, tactics, and inspiration.

When creating any sort of successful business model, the intense focus is going to be on a common issue that other people have. When creating your business, you are coming up with solutions for customers who seek to solve a problem that they have. You can pull this from inspiration from your own experiences. For example, somebody who struggled as a teen with sensitive skin might want to create and sell their line of natural soaps. Individuals who have had a disability might want to pursue a career where they try to help develop products to assist with that disability. By finding a problem and offering a great solution, that is where your success can genuinely lie.

What is missing? Often stories are inspired by those who are seeking to find that missing piece. How can you change people's lives? Be inventive and creative; don't just mimic or copy other people. Another spin on that original product idea is you can choose to make or market a product type that is already available. Remember, you or I may not invent something lifechanging. It may be you will sell a better line of home-baked bread, make a new custom-designed candle line, or market a great existing product already made and ready to sell.

P.S. Search the web for white label products. If you find a great product or line of products, you can set the goal of being a great marketer by adding your design, logo, and marketing plan. You know they do not make those products that celebrities sell, they are made for them. Companies in the U.S. and China will create for you original merchandise, and if you can imagine a great product, it can probably be produced. Some examples are kitchen utensils that are a bit different after your design input, pet products, eco-friendly bamboo plates, and many more.

Finding Inspiration

To find more inspirational ideas, there are many things you can do. Seek out these opportunities, just like you would with learning. First and foremost, start by watching inspirational movies and T.V. shows. Listen to inspirational music. These artistic outlets can help trigger certain creative aspects within you. You can watch documentaries and biographies about people who struggled.

Write out your feelings, and the inspiration exists inside of you. Write down the things that you can eliminate or that hold you back. Write down the things that you are adding in their place to bring those inspirational thoughts; you can get deep into your thoughts and dream of the changes, and write them down. Navigate what motivates you, and confront the significant struggles and issues that you have. Do you have a fear of failure? Are you worried about what other people are going to think about you? Are you struggling because you don't believe in yourself? Any of these things might be buried deep inside your mind, and maybe you don't even realize it because it feels so typical for you. Having low confidence and lacking self-esteem might be something that you are used to because it's just been for years. You can overcome this by journaling and even seeking out other ways to help you through this process. Many people have had lifechanging decisions brought about by their clear thinking brought about through meditation. Meditation is nothing crazy; it is just a way to clear your mind and help you eliminate hesitations, distractions, and the excuses that tag along with them.

Doing any one of these things can unlock a new part of your heart and mind, where that inspiration and those creative ideas are hiding.

Need inspiration? Change up your scenery by planning to visit heartening locations. If you find yourself staring at that blank wall again, that probably won't be where you will come up with your most robust ideas.

Go for a walk in the park. Find a body of water. Staring at the big blue sea and hearing the waves hit the rocks can just fill you with this more natural and intrinsic inspiring nature. For relaxation and inspiration, go to a botanical garden, visit the zoo, go to a friend's house or visit an art museum.

By changing up where you are physically and putting yourself in a refreshing place, your heart and mind will surely feel refreshed. As you're navigating throughout your daily life, set small goals for yourself. Of course, we all want to hit those huge milestones, but it's those small wins along the way that can make you more confident in yourself. Remember, small wins will add up to big wins. For example, if you're hoping to lose twenty pounds, set small milestones, and celebrate each time that you lose five. If you wait to celebrate until you hit that twenty-pound mark, that will be months away, and it can feel defeating to see your progress. Once you hit that five-pound mark, have mini-celebrations by giving yourself applause, buying a new outfit, or just doing anything that makes you feel good about yourself. By including these smaller celebrations of breakthroughs in your life, it becomes much easier to continue to feel motivated. The more successes that you can see, the easier it is to know within yourself that you are capable of fulfilling the goals you are setting.

Strength in Knowledge

You know that there is strength in knowledge, and sometimes learning can feel quite exhausting. It is fine to want to take a break, but remember that you should never stop learning. Always be open to new things and be willing to ask questions. Perhaps it can be scary to ask questions because you may be afraid that someone will judge you. If that's the case, really question why they would be judging you. Why would anybody shame another person for wanting to learn more? Anyone who tries to make you feel bad about your level of information may struggle with some insecurities of their own. Ignore them because another person's opinion should never keep you from an educational opportunity.

Encouragement is often found by gaining information. When do you feel most confident? When are you the least likely to make mistakes? Usually, these moments are fueled by the comfort we have with the knowledge that we have acquired. Please do not underestimate the power of all the resources we have reviewed, such as the free college courses, Udemy, and yes, even

YouTube. The more you know, the less likely you'll have as many speed bumps as you reach your future success. That includes continuing to find knowledge from those needed "how-to" guides and picking up on stories from people who have already experienced things that you have not.

Never be afraid to ask questions. If you don't understand something, you should speak up. Don't just pretend or fake your way through conversations because you're afraid of how you will look. Most people enjoy sharing their thoughts and knowledge with others, and if you know you have found a great resource in them, make a true friend and ask if you can stay in touch.

One challenge that you can give to yourself is to journal about one new thing that you learned every day. By logging the information and actions you come across, you will be able to reflect on everything you've learned throughout your journey. You can journal about specific categories as well. Pick one new thing that you learned about yourself. Pick one new thing that you learned about any business ideas. Pick one new thing that you learned about your family or a friend. Perhaps add a bit of variety to your journal and add one new thing that you learned about science, history, or love. You can go through the latest information you have learned and possibly even apply some of them to your new venture and your life in general.

Question: Do you already have a journal, or could you add it to your shopping list right now and start with a few entries today?

Chapter 9:

Home Sweet Home or Life on the Road?

When running with an idea, it's good to travel down all avenues to ensure that you're genuinely thinking everything through.

So what will it be: home sweet home or life on the road?

Which do you automatically find more appealing, money, opportunity, and responsibilities aside? Do you plan to master a talent from your garage, or is it your car that's going to be your business location of choice? The importance of questions like these matter, because it could make visualizing all the best possibilities clearer.

Taking the company you start on the road means that you might not always have a steady income. Travel-based businesses, like food trucks, can be one of the most challenging companies of all. There are many more risks when you travel as well. You will need to maintain your vehicle, possibly pay for major repairs at some point, and you or an employee could even get into a car accident. Businesses involved with delivering goods, services, or people where they need to go will need appropriate and reliable transportation. There could be times, mainly depending on your location that you will be subject to extreme weather conditions that you will need to plan for. You will need to have a back-up plan if your business gets moving as it were, and your transportation is not.

There are many conveniences in working from home. However, remaining home to work itself may also present some specific challenges. Some people may begin to feel cooped up and could even struggle to come up with inspiration. Opportunities for meeting other people and business connections will be limited. Learning information from home is limited to using the internet, books, and television for the most part. You might simply struggle to find motivation and end up procrastinating on your work all day. There are many benefits and challenges to either of these situations, so it's best to consider what could work best for you as you seek new opportunities.

The Convenience of a Home-Based Business

A home-based business can be more convenient because you'll likely have more time with your family. There are fewer upfront costs, you get to take breaks as you need to, and you might even be able to receive breaks on your taxes. The main benefit of working from home is that you would have more freedom. You set the plans in motion and schedule tasks to fit you and your potential clients. Perhaps you will be able to wake up when you plan to, and you get to work when you want to as well. You decide how many hours you need to put in, and there's no one breathing down your neck to get specific tasks done, except yourself.

Your cost savings can be huge, rather than paying for an office or a storefront, you'd only be paying your standard rent or mortgage. If you have a completely separate space and can dedicate an entire room to an office, you'll likely be able to claim some of your rent or mortgage on your income taxes. You will want to save all, and I mean all receipts to record business expenses to reduce your tax liability when Uncle Sam puts out his hand to collect. Remember to get tax and business start-up advice early. Use your journal (did you get one yet?), and as I said, learn enough accounting to understand the basics even if you have some help with your books.

Like previously mentioned, staying at home can be satisfying because it means that you could spend more time with your family. If you have one, you can work right next to your partner. People who have children can watch them play nearby while they are working away. If you have one, you could have a pet sit nearby or on your lap. Working from home is quite comforting if you can multitask. You could watch TV, listen to music, and use your phone as you need to while working. You can save time and money from eliminating a daily commute, while still being able to leave to pick up a coworker, a family member, or run errands.

However, there are also many potential disadvantages of working from home so you must be careful and prepared. One of the biggest ones is that it becomes challenging to navigate the differences between your work and your home life. Both aspects of their lives end up becoming blended, which means that they never genuinely feel clocked out. The ideas are always going to be flowing, and at any moment, you can walk into your office and pick up work. For the workaholic, this can be very bad. You might not want to sit down and get the job done, and instead, feel like you must go and finish household chores. Are you a person built for this, and could you honestly not get distracted often by the various happenings around your home? I know people who can listen to music while doing written assignments while I could never do that properly. These stay at home conveniences can be very satisfying, just make sure that you set yourself up for success, not distractions.

Possibilities At Home

Planning to keep the separation between your work and home life is one of the most challenging aspects of starting a home-based business.

The first and most important thing to do if you're working from home is to create boundaries. Let's say that you're married with two kids. Your spouse still has to go to work every day, but you're starting a home-based business where you sell customizable merchandise on Etsy. Your spouse might not think that you are working as hard anymore. Sometimes it can be easy for your partner to believe the one who stays home also has to take on the roles of the homemaker. Often we think that the person who's usually around the house is the one doing the cooking, cleaning, and those other traditional roles.

Let any family members know that when you're in your office with the door closed, you will not be disturbed.

Maybe you can have a specific signal or a sign outside your work area. You can have a particular set of headphones and tell the kids, "Whenever mom or dad is wearing headphones, nobody is allowed to interrupt them."

You have to create these boundaries to set limitations and ensure that your work and family life aren't conflicting

. You also have to set boundaries for yourself, give yourself a cutoff time. It's okay to have a goal to finish the day's efforts, such as 6 pm. Maybe you end up going a little bit over because you're dialed into your workflow. However, you have to set a cutoff time after that no matter what, you will stop working. That could be something like 7:00 pm, perhaps when you're about to eat dinner. By setting that cutoff time, you ensure that you're not working 24 hours a day. You also have to set boundaries with yourself. A significant one is not to think about work and not feel guilty when you're not active with your business responsibilities.

It's a challenging balance, working from home because there is always something you could be doing for your business. When you work in a traditional setting for someone else, you clock out and have to leave the office for the day. You could potentially work through the night from any room at your home-based office if you want to. It's great to be motivated, but it is best to know how to manage this guilt before getting started. For example, let's say it's Friday afternoon, and you didn't get nearly as much work done as you thought you should. You don't want to spoil your well-earned weekend off by working even more, but you also feel guilty about not getting it done. The thing is, when we work from home, it's easier to blame ourselves. However, if you had an office job, then you wouldn't let that ruin your weekend. You would think, "Well, I'll just get to it on Monday." That's the same mentality that you should while working a home business to keep things organized, positive, and productive.

Create boundaries with friends and family as well. Sometimes it's hard with friends because they know that you're working from home. They might ask you to let's say watch their dog, or for a ride to an appointment, or just to stop in and ask you to go out to lunch because they know you are home. It's easy to get persuaded into these things because, yes, technically, you do have the freedom, but you shouldn't take advantage of that flexibility. Once you open that door, then it's hard to close it, so make sure that you are letting people know that just because you're working from home doesn't mean that you're not working.

As I mentioned earlier, muscle memory can play a massive part in your efficiency at work. Don't give in to the temptation to work in bed. Try to avoid working in the living room or the common areas where you wouldn't typically work. Find or create that separate office space, so as soon as you sit down in that chair, you know you are "at work," and you will be much more focused and productive.

Mobile Jobs

Besides potential home positions you can create for yourself, there are many mobile job opportunities out there for you and their own sets of benefits. If you go back through the book, we have listed a plethora of potential prospects, so I'm not going to get more into what those are now; instead, let's focus on the benefits.

Working from home can be hard at times. It can leave you feeling bored, anxious, and stressed out depending on your personality. By taking life on the road, it can be much easier to help you with the separation of your home and work responsibilities. Just as you do from home, make sure that you have a separate space if you plan on doing something like working out of, or even living from a mobile vehicle. Many people dream of having a food business, such as a food truck. They sound so fun and appealing, but it is a costly endeavor as well, you have many of the similar expenses with a food truck as you would owning a restaurant. Yes, the vehicle itself may be affordable, but outfitting it legally and adequately is a challenge. Some people are very motivated by this idea, and some can make it work. It takes a significant amount of time and dedication. People often spend around $30,000 for a van with minimal equipment to over $200,000 for the fanciest setups. You also need to find out where you can set up your business and how much it can cost. There are prime locations near ball fields and the like, but there may be no room there, and the city can have substantial fees for top spots. The lesson here, look before you leap.

One of the most challenging parts about taking life on the road is that you don't know what's going to happen. You can't always guarantee that you're going to get customers. If you have a storefront, it's easy to know who your clientele is, and you can pay attention to when your most popular periods are by tracking sales and time. If you are in a food truck, that's a lot harder because you're going to be traveling around to different areas.

What are you going to do if you park in a spot for a day and only have one sale? That could happen, especially when you are getting started and making adjustments and improvements to your business. It could also occur at a home-based business, of course. There are more upfront costs that you will also need to consider because you're taking life on the road. You also have to think about your space. Are you going to be able to work in a small mobile area? If you're considering working on the road with your partner, you have to question if the two of you are legitimately going to get along that entire time.

Mobile jobs are still enjoyable and allow for many opportunities as well. You will continuously have new learning experiences; you'll see things that you never could before. Mobile jobs aren't just food trucks, either. You could freelance. You could be a writer, a video editor, a photographer, or many other occupations and can still travel while making your livelihood. You don't have to have a full-time home business or a full-time business on the road. You could remain working at a regular job if you have one, and build a mobile company in your spare time. You may come up with a plan to do some work from home and some activity on the road. The most important thing is to remember to pursue what works best for your happiness and success.

Chapter 10:

Love it! Selection & Action

"Don't worry about being successful, but work toward being significant, and the success will naturally follow."
-- Oprah Winfrey (INC, n.d.).

Not doing anything at all is just as big of a decision as going forward with actionable steps.

So far, in this book, you may have your dream business in mind, while others might feel overwhelmed. I have shared many options, and I wonder, what have you decided to do, or what ideas and possibilities have you eliminated?

You don't want me to tell you precisely what avenue to take, of course. I can help provide the criteria to use so you can judge what will work best for you. Not only is this beneficial for you in taking the first steps, but it's also a way to ensure you will have continued success well into the future.

To narrow things down, let's start eliminating some aspects of side income opportunities. Write down everything that you cannot or absolutely will not do. Please take your time considering these as your best choice will unveil itself if you eliminate with care. Items to remove are aspects like:

- Work from home
- Work with the public
- Travel and work
- Invest money
- Work online
- Sell items
- Creative services

Once you remove unworkable choices, it becomes so much easier to figure out what new money-making activity you will love.

Question: If you woke up tomorrow in your dream life, what career would you have?

You might not be able to immediately pursue this full time, and you can work towards it in a starting role. For example, maybe you would want to wake up as a full-time artist who makes beautiful pottery, paintings, photographs, or kaleidoscopes. Right now, you would not be able to do that because income won't allow a complete changeover yet. Why not start a vlog about your art online, take your wares to local fairs, and begin to sell items on Etsy right now? On your blog, you can gain followers and future customers as well.

Once you have narrowed things down, the third step is to ensure that you consider the things that are at least possible. Starting a food truck could be appealing, but do you have enough money? List out the restrictions. These might include:

- Money (How much money do you need to have what you need to begin and do you have that money?)
- Location (Do you have location restrictions?)
- Opportunity (Is this possible to do tomorrow? The day after? If not, when?)
- Availability (Do you have access to the things you need?)
- Desirable audience (Will people buy what you're selling?)

By going through these three steps, you will be able to narrow things down and select precisely what you want to do as your side hustle. To recap, this narrowing process involves:

1. Narrowing down the things you don't like
2. Understanding your dreams and connecting them to what is possible
3. Identifying realistic roadblocks to ensure your endeavors are feasible

Common Doubts

"I knew that if I failed I wouldn't regret that, but I knew the one thing I might regret is not trying." -- Jeff Bezos (INC, n.d.)

You likely have a few ideas still brewing, but maybe doubts are also settling in. I have one essential thing to remind you of:

You can do this.

Yes, you will have moments where you feel doubtful. You will question, "Is this truly for me?" You will wonder what could have been if you should turn back.

The thing is, we often seek out comfort. You might have moments where you want to run back to your old job. Remember that this is the comfort factor inside you, telling you that this is your only option. In your heart, you know it certainly is not the case whatsoever.

I know that you can do this because I didn't write a book on impossible ideas. I took them from my own experiences, business acquaintances, and successful people that you and I know. These are real options where people begin a side job or even a full-time endeavor if they can. They plant their idea, water and fertilize it, and grow it to become successful in their chosen path.

Wherever you are, whoever you are, and whatever circumstances surround you, finding a new income stream is possible.

The doubts are going to come in, but you have to be prepared to fight them off. Remind yourself: Other people's opinions don't have to affect what you do. Everyone has setbacks, but that does not mean you will not succeed. Being afraid can be inspiring if you use that fear as fuel. Nobody else is going to take this step for you.

Confront these thoughts as they happen. Where did they come from, did someone from your childhood instill doubt in you? Were you taught from a young age that you're not good enough? Have you been continuously made to feel like a failure? Is your anxiety telling you that something isn't right?

Of course, trust your gut, but also know when it is just serving up unproductive anxiety.

Listen to your mind, trust your gut, and feel with your heart in this process. The best way to follow something you want is to know how to understand all three of these voices.

Knowing what each of these is trying to tell you will help you better understand how to adapt and conquer.

Remember that this is not necessarily easy, and making money or finding success rarely is. Something challenging does not have to be a negative experience by any means. You can learn, grow, and thrive, no matter how demanding a situation might be.

Solid Action Steps

"Success seems to be connected with action. Successful people keep moving. They make mistakes, but they don't quit." -- Conrad Hilton (INC, n.d.)

Nothing will feel better than taking the first step. Well, except for the first check you get, of course.

What happens next is in your hands. Making that initial decision and taking that first step by following your heart is now something you have to do.

Getting started is the first roadblock. It could be intimidating, but think about how much lies ahead! Finding that motivation and encouragement can be challenging, especially when it's up to you to provide it. Take it slow if you need to but stick to a plan that you put together on a calendar or a journal. No one is saying you have to find a new opportunity on your first day. Start with a plan outline, spruce up your resume if you are taking the path of working at a new or additional location, and do simple Google searches on your field of study. Life could begin to change overnight, but you don't have to force yourself hastily.

So now I leave you with one additional bit of advice. I have summarized the process and have created these five steps for you. I encourage you to take action now, at least that first step, immediately. Here is your overall game plan:

Step one: Which general path will you take, get a part-time job, or quit your current situation and go full-time into a new job or business start-up? Refer back to the first section of this book to figure out what starting point you want as you begin your side hustle.

Step two: Research this position. Is it something you want, or something you're hoping to do? Can you feasibly fit into this position, or are you banking on luck? R might your competitors be, and what are the most significant drawbacks that might stop someone from finding success?

Step three: Come up with your exit strategy for your current position. Are you quitting your job, asking for a raise, or going part-time? Gather the information necessary, and work through each potential situation to account for any roadblocks. How long is this going to take?

Step four: Gather the tools needed. Are you selling things online? Are you creating a portfolio and resume to apply for a new job? Draft up your business plan and create schedules. Plan your budget by using a chart or spreadsheet of your expenses, with a projection of how much you'll likely make and when.

Step five: Be a bit patient, but keep going and adjust your expectations as needed. Some things will only be learned through trial and error, but that is normal and happens to all successful people and businesses. As required, create options and back-up plans with ideas for modifications to the existing plan.

Above all else, remember that there will be some roadblocks, unexpected twists, and maybe even a moment of luck, or a temporary failure. All that you do will be a learning experience from which you will grow.

"Build your own dreams, or someone else will hire you to build theirs." -- Farrah Gray (INC, n.d.)

Conclusion

Everybody has a dream for their future. We all have a vision that we hope to create. One of the most defeating feelings is looking around your life and realizing that none of you are helping that goal. There's nothing more emotionally draining and just plain sad than being in a position that you know was not your chosen fate. Clocking in day after day at a job that you don't care for whatsoever can be soul-crushing. Having to give your time and effort for demands that you have no passion for while ignoring the things that you genuinely care about is not your path to happiness.

Life is long on days that you have to work, but short on days that we give to our passions. Time is fleeting, and you deserve to be working towards giving your time to your heartfelt desires.

Although we may not wake up tomorrow with our business ideas complete, what you will be able to do is find extra income that is needed, or work towards crafting a niche in which you are passionate. You can create a business where other people will want to play a part. You can absolutely wake up excited tomorrow morning about taking those first initial steps.

You deserve to be excited. You have worked so hard, and now it is your time to find that personal success and give yourself the permission and freedom to live it.

Nobody else is going to make these decisions for you. Everybody is out to make sure that their own needs are met. It's not that we live in a selfish world, but it is a competitive one where other people often place their interests first. That means that we cannot depend on somebody else to find our success for us.

Don't buy into the idea that this is quick and easy. Many people are willing to take advantage of excited and hopeful entrepreneurs like you and I. They understand that craving and that passion, so they will paint you a picture of tan easy solution that you might buy. Moving ahead, you must step forward and be true to yourself. Pull out your journal, notepad, or device to log your thoughts and initial steps, no matter how simple they may seem. Writing down "Eliminate some choices" is better than a blank sheet, and actually, you should celebrate when you eliminate the ones that won't fit in your life. Why? Because your success is in the remaining choices.

Where do you want to be five years from now, what would you hope to see in your life?

Time for a bit of a breather and a review:

Remember that it all starts with cutting your costs. Money is quite a bit about the mindset you have about it, the more money that you save, the more money that you are earning, in a sense.

Remember to review the situation that you currently have. While it may feel the sole reason that you are unhappy is your work environment or income, perhaps there is something else that you can change around a bit to make things work out well. Maybe you just need to find a different boss, not necessarily a different career choice.

Look for more. Many of us have felt like we hit points in our careers where we have plateaued. Not everybody can climb the ranks and become the next CEO of the company. Perhaps you have achieved quite a bit and now have hit the ceiling, and you don't see where staying in that position is going to be able to carry you any further. Consider going from full-time to part-time as an option while adding on your new endeavor. Look for add-ons or other ways to start or enhance business by teaching classes, writing books, or starting a blog.

Maybe going simpler is something that you would enjoy. Perhaps you're sick of the office life, and you want to get back behind a bar and serve people on the weekends.

There's no shame in this; some will place a negative association with service or labor jobs as if there's something that we need to avoid. You could certainly do any one of these jobs while also still starting your own side business.

The point is we do not need to have a fancy title or a business suit to wear. What does any of that matter if you're not truly happy and living a life that you genuinely enjoy?

Do you need to earn extra money quickly, or are you willing to wait while you grow something that takes longer? What are your needs versus your preferences? Is this something that you're hoping to start within the next month, or are you willing to invest more time and grow a business over the next year?

Please don't overlook the free resources we reviewed. Many sources of information can be precious channels for you.

Find inspiration in everything and everyone that surrounds you. Create a mentality of positivity and encouragement. Yes, things can be scary, but the fear of failure is always going to be more detrimental and damaging to your potential than failing. In fact, failing is one of the best ways to learn from your mistakes to ensure that you never make them again.

Consider your needs and remember, at the end of the day, love your choices. You might have doubts, but trust your gut, listen to your mind, and feel this new direction with your heart. Keep an open mind, and stick to your plan to make steady progress. Create structured and organized goals and check-in with them often to ensure that you are taking the right steps.

This is your life to live, and it's you who wakes up each day and gets to chart their course. It's you who owns your challenges, thoughts, and dreams. It's you who can now make those life-changing decisions about your new direction.

Look deep within yourself and find your heartfelt inner voice. That is who will move you forward to your success; they are there, and they are ready, and that is where the magic will be found. Gillian Carr

ABOUT THE AUTHOR

Gillian Carr is an entrepreneur, researcher, and author. She has successfully launched multiple side businesses as she raised two daughters who graduated from the University of Washington.

As an avid reader of United States History, she is writing various books on the subjects that have intrigued her most. Instead of being pigeon-holed into one genre, books that are being published by Gillian include a wide variety of topics.

Soon to be released books include "Secrets of Inspiring Women," portraying important women from history, a startup business book "Side Hustle Magic," where some readers may shape the ideas revealed into a new career, healthy recipe books and more. Watch for the latest from Gillian Carr coming soon to a "bookshelf" near you!

References

Adams, R.L. (2017). How To Start A Blog That Earns A Real Income. Retrieved from https://www.forbes.com/sites/robertadams/2017/03/12/how-to-start-a-blog-that-earns-a-real-income/#5f1a275d3357

Akhtar, A. & Premack, R. (2019). Your 30-Step Plan for Getting the Promotion You Want and Deserve. Retrieved from https://www.businessinsider.com/how-to-get-promoted-at-work-2018-7

Amazon. (n.d.). The Amazon Advantage. Retrieved from https://logistics.amazon.com/?utm_source=google&utm_medium=paid_search&utm_campaign=brand_delivery&utm_term=desktop

Ashley, E. (n.d.). Flea Market Flipping: Make Money Flipping Items For Profit. Retrieved from https://www.mintnotion.com/extra-income/flea-market-flipping-make-money-flipping-items-for-profit/

Boitnott, J. (n.d.). 25 Simple Ways for Entrepreneurs to Find Inspiration. Retrieved from https://www.inc.com/john-boitnott/25-

simple-ways-for-entrepreneurs-to-find-inspiration.html

Chegg Tutors. (n.d.). Online Tutoring Jobs. Retrieved from https://www.chegg.com/tutors/become-a-tutor/?from_header=1

Garner, S. (2015). Where Do Great Small Business Ideas Come From? Retrieved from http://canadianentrepreneurtraining.com/where-do-great-small-business-ideas-come-from/

Gregory, A. (2020). 1010 New Ideas to Inspire You to Start a Business. Retrieved from https://www.thebalancesmb.com/small-business-ideas-2951453

Gross, E. (2016). 8 Managers Share the Best Way to Ask for A Raise. Retrieved from https://www.forbes.com/sites/elanagross/2016/06/27/8-managers-share-the-best-way-to-ask-for-a-raise-and-get-it/#298955d174ff

Hamm, T. (2020). 40 Ways to Save Money on Monthly Expenses. Retrieved from https://www.thesimpledollar.com/save-money/trimming-the-fat-forty-ways-to-reduce-your-monthly-required-spending/

INC. (n.d.) 17 Motivational Quotes to Inspire Small-Business Owners. Retrieved from https://www.inc.com/peter-economy/17-

motivational-quotes-to-inspire-small-business-owners.html

Inveiss, N. (n.d.). How to Sell Printful Products on Etsy. Retrieved from https://www.printful.com/blog/how-to-sell-printful-products-on-etsy/

Jenkin, M. (2013). What inspired you to start a small business? Retrieved from https://www.theguardian.com/small-business-network/2013/jun/27/start-small-business-inspiration

Martucci, B. (n.d.). 26 Cost Cutting Ideas for Your Small Business to Reduce Expenses. Retrieved from https://www.moneycrashers.com/cost-cutting-ideas-small-business-expenses/

Meyer, S. (2017). 8 Insanely Profitable Skills You Can Learn For Free (And On Your Own Time). Retrieved from https://medium.com/swlh/8-insanely-profitable-skills-you-can-learn-for-free-and-on-your-own-time-134b5d9a6030

Morgaine, B. (n.d.) Origin Stories: 11 Moments That Inspired Entrepreneurs to Start Their Own Businesscs. Retrieved from https://articles.bplans.com/origin-stories-11-moments-that-inspired-entrepreneurs-to-start-their-own-businesses/

Prince, A. (2019). 25 Killer Sites For Free Online Education. Retrieved from https://www.lifehack.org/articles/money/25-killer-sites-for-free-online-education.html

Quinn, M. (2020). Need Money Now? 10 Ways To Make Money Fast. Retrieved from https://www.gobankingrates.com/money/side-gigs/ways-to-make-cash-quick/

Rapacon, S. (2020). Top 25 Part-Time Jobs for Retirees. Retrieved from https://www.aarp.org/work/job-search/info-2020/part-time-jobs-for-retirees.html

Reinstetle, M. (2020). Here Are the 10 Best Second Jobs. Retrieved from https://www.thepennyhoarder.com/make-money/side-gigs/best-second-jobs/

Scrivens, P. (n.d.). 9 Sites That Will Pay You to Browse the Internet. Retrieved from https://struggle.co/get-paid-test-websites/

Smith, J. (2013). 16 Mistakes Employees Make When Trying to Get a Promotion. Retrieved from https://www.forbes.com/sites/jacquelynsmith/2013/10/24/16-mistakes-employees-make-when-trying-to-get-a-promotion/#54896c5935f1

Snider, S. (2019). 10 Expenses Destroying Your Budget. Retrieved from https://money.usnews.com/money/personal-finance/saving-and-budgeting/slideshows/10-expenses-destroying-your-budget

Team Localwise. (n.d.). 38 Best Part-Time Jobs for College Students. Retrieved from https://www.localwise.com/a/100-38-best-part-time-jobs-for-college-students-updated-july-2019

The Balance Careers. (n.d.). 10 Steps to a Successful Career Change. Retrieved from https://www.thebalancecareers.com/successful-career-change-2058452

Wang, J. (2020). 7 Ways to Make Money With Your Car. Retrieved from https://wallethacks.com/how-to-make-money-with-your-car/

We Are Teachers Staff. (2020). 25 Ways Teachers Can Make Extra Money. Retrieved from https://www.weareteachers.com/ways-teachers-can-make-extra-money/

Your Dictionary. (n.d.). Who Said "A Penny Saved is a Penny Earned"? Retrieved from https://quotes.yourdictionary.com/articles/who-said-a-penny-saved-is-a-penny-earned.html

www.ingramcontent.com/pod-product-compliance
Lightning Source LLC
Chambersburg PA
CBHW052346220526
45465CB00003BA/985